Get the most from this book

KU-203-638

Everyone has to decide his or her own revision strategy, but it is essential to review your work, learn it and test your understanding. These Revision Notes will help you to do that in a planned way, topic by topic. Use this book as the cornerstone of your revision and don't hesitate to write in it — personalise your notes and check your progress by ticking off each section as you revise.

☑ **Tick to track your progress**

Use the revision planner on pages 4 and 5 to plan your revision, topic by topic. Tick each box when you have:

- revised and understood a topic
- tested yourself
- practised the exam questions and gone online to check your answers and complete the quick quizzes

You can also keep track of your revision by ticking off each topic heading in the book. You may find it helpful to add your own notes as you work through each topic.

My revision planner

Unit 3C Representative processes in the USA

	Revised	Tested	Exam ready
1 Elections and voting			
8 Presidential elections			
24 Congressional elections			
26 Propositions, referendums and recall elections			
2 Political parties			
29 Organisation of the two major parties			

Racial and ethnic diversity in the USA

Changes in the US population — Revised

In the beginning, the USA was a creation of white European Protestants. Black people were, in most cases, slaves; Native Americans were not regarded as citizens either. During the nineteenth and twentieth centuries all that changed.
- The end of the Civil War (1865) brought the emancipation of the slaves.
- Immigration through the nineteenth and twentieth centuries brought a flood of new settlers: Irish Catholics; European Jews; Hispanics from Mexico and other Central American countries; refugees from Africa, the Middle East and Asia.

Features to help you succeed

Examiner's tips

Throughout the book there are tips from the examiner to help you boost your final grade.

Definitions and key words

Clear, concise definitions of essential key terms are provided on the page where they appear.

Key words from the specification are highlighted in bold for you throughout the book.

Typical mistakes

The examiner identifies the typical mistakes candidates make and explains how you can avoid them.

Debates

Debates are highlighted to help you to assess arguments and use evidence appropriately.

Now test yourself

These short, knowledge-based questions provide the first step in testing your learning. Answers are at the end of the book.

Exam practice

Practice exam questions are provided for each topic. Use them to consolidate your revision and practise your exam skills.

Online

Go online to check and print out your answers to the exam questions and try out the extra quick quizzes at **www.therevisionbutton.co.uk/myrevisionnotes**

My revision planner

Exam practice answers and quick quizzes at **www.therevisionbutton.co.uk/myrevisionnotes**

Unit 4C Governing the USA

Exam practice answers and quick quizzes at **www.therevisionbutton.co.uk/myrevisionnotes**

Countdown to my exams

6–8 weeks to go

- Start by looking at the specification — make sure you know exactly what material you need to revise and the style of the examination. Use the revision planner on pages 4 and 5 to familiarise yourself with the topics.
- Organise your notes, making sure you have covered everything on the specification. The revision planner will help you to group your notes into topics.
- Work out a realistic revision plan that will allow you time for relaxation. Set aside days and times for all the subjects that you need to study, and stick to your timetable.
- Set yourself sensible targets. Break your revision down into focused sessions of around 40 minutes, divided by breaks. These Revision Notes organise the basic facts into short, memorable sections to make revising easier.

Revised ☐

4–6 weeks to go

- Read through the relevant sections of this book and refer to the examiner's tips, typical mistakes and key terms. Tick off the topics as you feel confident about them. Highlight those topics you find difficult and look at them again in detail.
- Test your understanding of each topic by working through the 'Now test yourself' questions in the book. Look up the answers at the back of the book.
- Make a note of any problem areas as you revise, and ask your teacher to go over these in class.
- Look at past papers. They are one of the best ways to revise and practise your exam skills. Write or prepare planned answers to the exam practice questions provided in this book. Check your answers online and try out the extra quick quizzes at **www.therevisionbutton.co.uk/ myrevisionnotes**
- Try different revision methods. For example, you can make notes using mind maps, spider diagrams or flash cards.
- Track your progress using the revision planner and give yourself a reward when you have achieved your target.

Revised ☐

One week to go

- Try to fit in at least one more timed practice of an entire past paper and seek feedback from your teacher, comparing your work closely with the mark scheme.
- Check the revision planner to make sure you haven't missed out any topics. Brush up on any areas of difficulty by talking them over with a friend or getting help from your teacher.
- Attend any revision classes put on by your teacher. Remember, he or she is an expert at preparing people for examinations.

Revised ☐

The day before the examination

- Flick through these Revision Notes for useful reminders, for example the examiner's tips, typical mistakes and key terms.
- Check the time and place of your examination.
- Make sure you have everything you need — extra pens and pencils, tissues, a watch, bottled water, sweets.
- Allow some time to relax and have an early night to ensure you are fresh and alert for the examinations.

Revised ☐

My exams

A2 US Government & Politics Unit 3C

Date: ....

Time: ....

Location: ....

A2 US Government & Politics Unit 4C

Date: ....

Time: ....

Location: ....

Exam practice answers and quick quizzes at **www.therevisionbutton.co.uk/myrevisionnotes**

Examiner's summary

Both the papers you will sit last 90 minutes. In each paper, you must answer:

- three out of five short answer questions (worth 15 marks each)
- one out of three long answer questions (worth 45 marks)

So there are 90 marks to be gained in 90 minutes — a mark per minute. You should therefore spend no more than 15 minutes on each of the three short answer questions, and make sure you have at least 45 minutes to write the one long answer.

Your answers will be marked according to:

- knowledge and understanding (30%)
- analysis and evaluation (50%)
- communication and language (20%)

So answers that merely reel off the facts (knowledge and understanding) will not get you far at this level. Half the marks for each answer will be awarded for analysis and evaluation. Many questions will contain a command word indicating what the examiner wants you to do to answer a particular question, for example:

- analyse
- assess
- discuss
- evaluate
- explain

Don't get too tied up about the differences between each word: essentially they are all asking you to present an argument. Sometimes the question may contain an important phrase, such as:

- How effective is/are…
- To what extent is/are…

So you might be asked: 'How effective are the checks and balances between the president and Congress?' Don't just list the checks and balances and give examples — though you do need to do both of those things — make sure that for each check, you discuss its effectiveness.

Similarly, you might be asked: 'To what extent does the president control US foreign policy?' Again, it is not enough merely to go through the president's foreign policy powers. A debate is being asked for, because if the president is not in control, then someone/ something else must be, so you need to evaluate the extent of the president's control as opposed to control by Congress, the courts, public opinion or whatever.

Be prepared to demonstrate an understanding of the extent of debate and disagreement over the nature, development and workings of the US political system (synopticity). Think in terms of 'arguments for and against', 'pros and cons', or 'strengths and weaknesses' when considering any area that promotes debate or

disagreement, for example presidential primaries or affirmative action programmes.

Ensure that you 'answer the question'. Ask yourself:

- Is there anything in the question that requires definition, clarification or explanation?
- What is the key word or phrase in the question?

You will often need to begin your answer by defining, clarifying or explaining things. For example, imagine you are responding to the question: 'Examine the claim that the process for selecting presidential candidates is undemocratic.' You will need to explain the process for selecting presidential candidates and what the word 'undemocratic' means. Only then can you answer the question.

The key word or phrase in the question should be used as the focus for your answer. So in the example just given, the key word is 'undemocratic'. The best answers will be organised along the following lines:

1. an explanation of 'the process for selecting presidential candidates'
2. a definition/clarification of the term 'undemocratic'
3. arguments to support the claim
4. arguments against the claim

Remember, the recipe for good essays at this level is logical argument backed up by relevant, up-to-date examples.

Pitfalls to avoid

- This book is divided into eight distinct topics, but don't think of these topics as eight separate compartments. They should be read and understood together. For example, don't just think about pressure groups, but about how pressure groups interact with Congress, the executive and the Supreme Court.

- When you look at the questions on the exam paper, don't think, 'This is the Congress question', or 'This is the Constitution question'. The exam may include some questions that ask about only one topic but equally the examiner may ask questions that require you to draw material from two or more topics.

- As an examiner, I once asked the question: 'Why has the US Constitution been so rarely amended?' After the exam, some teachers complained that there were no questions relating to the Supreme Court. Even these *teachers* had failed to spot that a significant part of the answer to this question was about the Supreme Court's power of judicial review.

- Don't go into lengthy background material. In answer to the question mentioned above, one candidate wrote a seven-page answer. But four pages were just background on the writing of the Constitution itself, which wasn't relevant to the question.

- Wherever possible, illustrate your answers with relevant, up-to-date examples.

1 Elections and voting

Presidential elections

Presidential elections occur:

- every 4 years
- in years divisible by 4: 2004, 2008, 2012, 2016, etc.
- on the Tuesday after the first Monday in November (i.e. between 2 November and 8 November)

The Constitution (Article II) states that to be eligible to be president a person must:

- be a natural-born US citizen
- be at least 35 years of age
- have been resident in the USA for at least 14 years

The Constitution (Amendment XXII, 1951) also states that a person cannot serve more than two terms as president.

A presidential election can be thought of as occurring in four stages. The first two are concerned with *choosing the candidates*; the second two are concerned with *electing the president* (see Table 1.1)

> **Examiner's tip**
>
> In exam questions do be careful to see the difference between the phrases 'selecting presidential candidates' and 'electing the president'.

Table 1.1 Presidential elections: a four-stage process

Stage	Functions	Occurs
1 Primaries and caucuses	(i) Show popularity of candidates (ii) Choose delegates to attend the National Party Conventions	January–June
2 National Party Conventions	(i) Choose presidential candidate (ii) Choose vice-presidential candidate (iii) Decide on party platform	July–August /early September (each lasts 4 days)
3 General election campaign	The campaign between candidates of the various parties	September, October, first week of November
4 Election Day and Electoral College	Elect the president and vice-president through the Electoral College	Election Day: Tuesday after the first Monday in November Electoral College votes: Monday after the second Wednesday in December

> **Now test yourself**
>
> 1 How often do presidential elections occur?
>
> 2 What are the three constitutional requirements to be president?
>
> 3 What does the 22nd Amendment state about the number of terms a president may serve?
>
> Tested

Primaries

Revised ☐

Definitions

A **presidential primary** is an election to select a party's candidate for the presidency. Some states with a small population spread over a large geographic area often hold **caucuses** instead of a primary. The states that held caucuses rather than a primary in 2008 included Iowa, Wyoming, North Dakota, Minnesota and Nevada.

A **presidential primary** is an election to select a party's candidate for the presidency.

A **caucus** is a meeting to select a party's candidate for the presidency.

Functions

Presidential primaries have two main functions:

1 to show the popularity of presidential candidates

2 to choose delegates to go to the National Party Conventions

How primaries are run

Presidential primaries are run under *state* law, not federal law. That means there are potentially 50 different ways of running primaries, which is confusing. Just keep to the main rules of thumb. You need to know that states decide *six* important things about primaries:

1 *Whether to hold a primary or a caucus.* The vast majority of states now hold primaries.

2 *When to hold the primary.* Primaries tend to be held between January and June. But each state will decide exactly when within that 4–5-month period to schedule their primary: whether to go early or late, to go for a date on their own or to coincide it with other, maybe neighbouring, states.

3 *How to conduct the primary.* Recently, some states have experimented with postal voting and electronic voting via the internet.

4 *Who can vote in the primary.* It is important to understand that any registered voter can vote in a primary in any state. But in some states, when you register you are asked to declare your party affiliation — whether you consider yourself to be a Democrat or Republican. Some states then allow only registered Democrats to vote in the Democratic primary and only registered Republicans to vote in the Republican primary. This is known as a **closed primary**. Other states don't bother with establishing party affiliation. They allow any registered voter to decide, on the day of the primary, whether they want to vote in the Democratic primary or the Republican primary. This is known as an **open primary**.

5 *Who can be on the ballot.* States have their own laws about who gets on the ballot. In some states, notably New York, these are strange indeed and often keep serious, well-known candidates off the ballot.

6 *How to allocate the delegates.* In most primaries, candidates are awarded delegates in proportion to the votes they get. This is known as a **proportional primary**. Most states set a threshold — a minimum percentage of votes that a candidate must receive to get any of that state's delegates. The threshold is usually 15% of the vote. However, in some Republican primaries, whoever gets the most votes wins all that state's delegates to the National Party Convention. This is known as a **winner-takes-all primary**. The Democratic Party forbids them, so all its primaries are proportional primaries.

Examiner's tip

In answers, having quickly made the distinction between primaries and caucuses, you can use the term 'primaries', as that is what the vast majority of states hold nowadays.

Typical mistakes

Don't use the term 'proportional representation'; it isn't. Proportional representation refers to a particular type of electoral system that is not used in the USA.

Front loading

As primaries have become more and more important, states have tried to make their primary more prominent and influential by moving the date earlier in the year. This is called **front loading**.

The number of states holding their primaries or caucuses before the end of March increased from just 11 in 1980 to 42 by 2008. And those 42 states included all eight of the largest states, such as New York, Texas and California. California has moved from early June in 1980 to early February in 2008. New York has moved from mid-April to early February. By 5 February 2008, 55% of the delegates to the Democratic and Republican Conventions had already been chosen. Front loading has also given rise to another phenomenon, that of **Super Tuesday**.

> **Front loading** is the phenomenon by which states schedule their presidential primaries or caucuses earlier in the cycle in an attempt to increase their importance in the choosing of candidates.
>
> **Super Tuesday** is a day, often in early February, when a large number of states hold their primaries or caucuses.

The invisible primary

Front loading has increased the importance of another phenomenon — the **invisible primary**.

The so-called invisible primary begins almost immediately after the previous presidential election and lasts through to the holding of the first primary and caucus of the election year. It is called 'invisible' because few scheduled events are held during this period. There is therefore nothing (or very little) to see. It is a time when would-be candidates:

> **Invisible primary** is the year or so before the start of the primaries when potential candidates try to gain recognition and money as well as put together the necessary organisation.

- try to get 'mentioned' in the serious press — newspapers like the *Washington Post* and the *New York Times*
- try to get coverage on television programmes like *The NewsHour* with Jim Lehrer on PBS
- set up exploratory committees
- visit key primary and caucus states such as New Hampshire and Iowa

and then, eventually:

- start fundraising
- put together a prospective campaign staff
- formally announce their candidacy for the presidency

Because the primary season itself is now so short — in 2004 both George W. Bush and John Kerry had made certain of their party's nomination by 2 March — there is no longer any time to build name recognition, momentum and money during the primaries. So one has to do it *before* then — during the invisible primary.

This means campaigns start much earlier. For example:

- 1960: Senator John F. Kennedy announced he was running for the presidency on 2 January of that year, *66 days* before the first primary.
- 2008: Senator Barack Obama announced he was running for the presidency *332 days* before the first primary.

There is also much evidence to suggest that this is a most important stage. For example:

- Since 1988, the Republicans have nominated as their candidate the person who was ahead in the opinion polls at the end of the invisible primary on five out of six occasions.

- Since 1988, the Democrats have nominated as their candidate the person who was ahead in the opinion polls at the end of the invisible primary on three of those six occasions.

20366
THOMAS TALLIS
SCHOOL LIBRARY

Advantages and disadvantages of primaries

Revised

Advantages of primaries	Disadvantages of primaries
(1) Increased level of participation by ordinary voters: 30% in 2008	(1) Turnout is usually low: less than 20% of eligible voters (though not in 2008)
(2) Increased level of interest: e.g. in Democratic race in 2008	(2) Voters are unrepresentative of typical general election voters: more elderly, more ideological, better educated, more wealthy
(3) Increased choice of candidates: up to 14 in 2008	(3) Makes the process far too long, which may discourage some better-qualified candidates from running
(4) Opening up the process to 'outsider' candidates: e.g. Bill Clinton (1992), Obama (2008)	(4) Too expensive and media orientated
(5) Removing power of the party bosses	(5) Bitter personal battles can develop: e.g. Obama and Hillary Clinton (2008)
(6) Significantly diminishing opportunities for corruption by doing away with the old 'smoke-filled rooms'	(6) Fails to test a number of important presidential qualities
(7) Weeding out candidates not up to the gruelling contest	(7) Lacks significant input from professional politicians, with too much power being given to ordinary voters

Debate

Advantages and disadvantages of primaries

Possible further reform

Revised

Criticism of the current system of primaries has led to calls for further reform. Proposals tend to fall into a number of categories:

- a national primary
- a series of four regional primaries: the Northeast, the South, the Midwest and the West
- further limits on money raising and spending
- a pre-primary mini-convention to choose the shortlist of candidates who would then run in the primaries
- states voting in order of size of population, beginning with the smallest

There are four problems with these possible reforms:

1. The National Committees and Conventions of both parties would have to agree to the same reform.
2. All 50 states would have to agree to change their state laws.
3. A number of states strongly favour the current system over any of the proposals above.
4. Further limiting money raising and spending would require an Act of Congress which would not be deemed by the Supreme Court as unconstitutional (see p. 100).

Now test yourself

4. What is the difference between a primary and a caucus?
5. What are the two functions of primaries?
6. What is the difference between an open and a closed primary?
7. What is the difference between a proportional and a winner-takes-all primary?
8. What is front loading?
9. What is the invisible primary?
10. What are the advantages and disadvantages of primaries?

Tested

National Party Conventions

The staging of National Party Conventions

Each of the major parties — and some minor parties — hold a **National Party Convention**. They are:

- held in the summer of the presidential election year (July/August/early September) and usually last for 4 days
- held in a large city: in 2012, the Republicans in Tampa (Florida) and the Democrats in Charlotte (North Carolina)
- held at a venue decided by each party's National Committee
- attended by delegates (most of them chosen in the primaries) and the media

> A **National Party Convention** is a meeting held once every 4 years by each party to select its presidential and vice-presidential candidates and finalise a party platform.

Formal functions of National Party Conventions

The National Party Conventions are said to have three formal functions:

1 to choose the presidential candidate

2 to choose the vice-presidential candidate

3 to decide on the party platform (that is, the policy document or 'manifesto')

Choosing the presidential candidate

This function has been lost almost entirely to the primaries. Almost all of the delegates who attend the Conventions are nowadays chosen in the primaries. They are chosen as 'committed delegates' — committed to voting for their candidate on the first ballot at the Convention if he or she is still in the race.

To win the presidential nomination, a candidate must receive an absolute majority of the delegate votes. In 2008, there were 4,418 delegates attending the Democratic National Convention. Barack Obama therefore needed 2,210 votes to win the nomination. Once he had won that number of committed delegates — which he eventually achieved by early June — he was the certain nominee of his party, over 2 months before the Democratic National Convention met at the end of August.

It is therefore more accurate to say that the Convention merely confirms rather than chooses the presidential candidate. Not since the Republican Convention of 1976 has the choice of the presidential candidate really been in any doubt at the opening of the Convention. In that year, President Gerald Ford defeated ex-Governor Ronald Reagan by 1,187 delegate votes to 1,070.

Choosing the vice-presidential candidate

This function has also been lost. Not since 1956 has a National Convention actually chosen the vice-presidential candidate, known as the **running-mate**. Nowadays, the running-mate is chosen by the presidential candidate. Indeed, in recent years the announcement of the running-mate has been made *before* rather than *at* the National Convention. In 2008, both Barack Obama and John McCain announced their running-mates — Joe Biden and Sarah Palin respectively — just

> **Typical mistakes**
>
> Avoid the common error of candidates who state that the Conventions 'choose the president' and 'choose the vice-president'. They don't. They choose the presidential and vice-presidential *candidates*.

> **Examiner's tip**
>
> Don't worry too much about who the delegates are and exactly how they are chosen. Examiners will not expect that level of detail.

Exam practice answers and quick quizzes at **www.therevisionbutton.co.uk/myrevisionnotes**

before their Conventions convened. It is therefore more accurate to state that the Convention merely *confirms* rather than *chooses* the vice-presidential candidate.

In choosing the vice-presidential candidate, the presidential candidate often looks for a **balanced ticket**. This means choosing a running-mate who is different from them in terms of:

- geographic region of origin or residence
- political experience
- age
- and maybe: gender, race, religion

A good example of a 'balanced ticket' would be the Republican ticket in 2008 of John McCain and Sarah Palin. This is shown in Table 1.2.

Table 1.2 A balanced ticket: McCain–Palin, 2008

Characteristic	John McCain	Sarah Palin
Political experience	US Congress	State Governor
Gender	Male	Female
Geographic region	Southwest (Arizona)	Alaska
Age	72	44
Ideology	Moderate Republican	Conservative Republican

Deciding on the party platform

The **party platform** is the document containing the policies that the party intends to follow if it wins the election.

The platform is put together by the platform committee under the direction of the party's national committee. The platform committee holds hearings around the country during the first 6 months of the election year. A draft platform is presented to delegates at the beginning of the Convention. There may then be debates on various planks (parts) of the platform. But nowadays, parties try to avoid heated and contentious debates at the Convention. They feel it makes the party look divided — like the Republican Convention in 1992, in its disagreement over abortion.

> **Party platform** is the statement of a party's policies for an upcoming presidential election.

Informal functions of National Party Conventions

Revised

The Conventions are said to have three *informal* functions:

1 to promote party unity
2 to enthuse the party faithful
3 to enthuse the ordinary voters

Promoting party unity

Promoting party unity is an important function of the Conventions because:

- the Convention is the only time in 4 years that the party actually meets together; at other times, the party exists merely as 50 state parties

- any wounds created in the primaries can be healed
- it gives the defeated candidates an opportunity to support the chosen candidate publicly (e.g. Hillary Clinton supporting Barack Obama at the 2008 Democratic Convention)

The media will comment on whether or not the party is united. Disunited Conventions usually lead to defeat at the general election (e.g. Republicans 1992; Democrats 1980).

Enthusing the party faithful

The 'party faithful' are the delegates. It is important that they are 'enthused' by the candidates and the platform because:

- they are the people who will be organising and carrying out much of the campaigning at a state and local level
- they need to communicate that enthusiasm to ordinary voters in their own communities
- they therefore need to believe that they have a winning ticket and winning policies

Enthusing ordinary voters

The 'ordinary voters', of course, are not at the Convention. It is through television that the parties will hope to communicate with them, and especially through the media coverage of the presidential candidate's **acceptance speech** on the last night of the Convention. This speech is important because:

- it is the first opportunity for the presidential candidate to address ordinary voters
- the candidate will hope to display presidential qualities to voters
- the candidate will give an outline of the policies to be addressed
- the candidate will hope to boost their opinion poll ratings as a direct result — what is called '**bounce**'

This was especially important for Obama in 2008 because typical American voters knew little about him.

> **Examiner's tip**
>
> To help you with questions that ask you for arguments for and against the claim that National Party Conventions are/are not any longer important, construct a two-column table, putting arguments for on one side and arguments against on the other.

Importance of modern-day Conventions
Revised

Many commentators suggest that, in comparison to Conventions of years ago, modern-day Conventions are of little importance because:

- the presidential candidates are chosen in the primaries
- the vice-presidential candidates are chosen by the presidential candidates and announced before the Convention
- the parties try to lay on 'scripted' and 'sanitised' Conventions, devoid of controversy and hence of interest
- the terrestrial (as opposed to the cable) television companies give much less coverage to the Conventions

However, Conventions should not be too easily written off. While the formal functions may have declined in importance, the informal functions are still important. As presidential election scholar Stephen Wayne puts it, the Conventions 'may have become less newsworthy, but they are still important'.

> **Now test yourself**
>
> 11 What are the three formal functions of National Party Conventions?
>
> 12 What is meant by a 'balanced ticket'?
>
> 13 What is the party platform?
>
> 14 What are the three informal functions of the National Party Conventions?
>
> 15 Give three reasons why the presidential candidate's acceptance speech is important.
>
> *Tested*

Exam practice answers and quick quizzes at **www.therevisionbutton.co.uk/myrevisionnotes**

The general election campaign

Revised

The general election:

- is when the **intra-party** campaign has finished and the **inter-party** campaign begins
- by tradition begins on Labor Day — the first Monday in September
- runs for 8–9 weeks until the day before election day in early November
- is expensive
- is conducted largely on television
- includes the televised presidential debates — usually three of them during October — plus one televised debate between the two vice-presidential candidates (see p. 17)

The candidates tour the country, spending time in states that have large numbers of Electoral College votes and/or which are seen as 'swing' states: that is, could be won by either party.

> **Now test yourself**
>
> 16 When does the general election campaign traditionally begin?
>
> 17 What is the difference between the 'intra-party' and 'inter-party' campaigns?
>
> 18 How long does the general election campaign last?
>
> 19 In which medium is the campaign mainly conducted?
>
> Tested

Campaign finance pre-reforms

Revised

US election campaigns are often criticised for spending vast sums of money. Such criticism may well have merit, but it is important to remember some of the reasons why US elections are so expensive, especially when compared with UK parliamentary elections:

- The country is vast (the entire UK is the size of Oregon).
- The elections are not just to elect one legislative chamber (as in the UK).
- The general election campaign lasts 9 weeks, not 3–4 weeks as in the UK.
- Candidates must contest the primaries, which begin 9 months before Election Day.
- There is no 'free time' on US television; buying time is expensive.

Until the 1970s, campaign finance was largely unregulated, which meant that:

- personal wealth was important in running for political office (e.g. JFK in 1960)
- people were not limited in the sums they could give to candidates
- 'fat cats' gave huge sums (often running into millions of dollars) to candidates
- candidates were not limited in the sums they could spend on their campaigns
- many opportunities for corruption existed

> **Typical mistakes**
>
> Be careful when writing about the importance of money. It is misleading to say that someone 'needs a lot of money' to run for the presidency. That could be taken to mean that you have to be personally wealthy. Say, rather, that someone 'needs to raise a lot of money' to run for the presidency.

Campaign finance: 2002 reforms

Revised

But the 1970s reforms left a number of loopholes, which became new and significant problems during the elections of the 1980s and 1990s. These included problems concerning:

- 'soft money' spent by political parties on 'party building' or 'get-out-the-vote' activities
- the growth in 'issue advocacy' campaigning by, for example, abortion, environmental and labour union groups

- the weakening of parties as 'matching funds' go directly to the candidates' organisations rather than to the parties
- the failure of the Federal Election Commission to have much in the way of enforcement powers against those who break the new rules

Following the campaign finance abuses surrounding Bill Clinton's re-election campaign in 1996, Republican Senator John McCain and Democrat Senator Russell Feingold were successful in getting another raft of reforms passed through Congress in 2002.

The principal changes brought about by the 2002 reforms were:

- National Party Committees banned from raising or spending 'soft money'
- labour unions and corporate groups forbidden from directly funding issue advertisements
- the banning of union or corporate money to fund advertisements that mention a federal candidate, within 60 days of a general election or 30 days of a primary
- the prohibition of fundraising on federal property
- increased individual limits on contributions to individual candidates or candidate committees to $2,300 (2007–08), to be further increased for inflation in each odd-numbered year
- the banning of contributions from foreign nationals
- 'Stand By Your Ad' provision, resulting in all campaign ads including a verbal endorsement by the candidate with the words: 'I'm [candidate's name] and I approve this message'

Examiner's tip

To help with questions that ask you for strengths and weaknesses of the current state of campaign finance reform, construct a two-column table, putting strengths on one side and weaknesses on the other.

Now test yourself

20 Which two senators were responsible for introducing the campaign finance reforms of 2002?

21 Make a list of the principal changes brought about by the 2002 reforms.

Tested

The media

Revised

The term 'the media' includes print journalism, radio and television, though television is the most important in this context.

Newspapers

There are no national titles, except for *USA Today* (a weekday broadsheet) and the *Wall Street Journal* (the US equivalent of the UK's *Financial Times*). But there are local papers that have a national reputation, such as the *Washington Post* and the *New York Times*. What is most important is what the columnists in these kinds of papers say in their opinion pages as well as the endorsements they make of particular candidates near to Election Day. Don't forget also the websites that these and other newspapers now maintain.

Journals

These are weeklies aimed at a general readership. The main titles are *Time* and *Newsweek*. 'Cover stories' are the most important factor of these journals: that is, the inside story which features on the cover of that week's edition. Again, related websites are now used extensively.

Television

Different types and forms of television
Television is the principal medium for imparting information during a US election. It exists in two forms:

1 terrestrial — the 'networks': ABC, CBS, NBC and PBS
2 cable: CNN, Fox News, MSNBC and C-SPAN

Television carries mainly three different forms of political information and coverage:

1 daily news programmes: e.g. ABC's *Good Morning America* and *World News*

2 nightly documentary programmes: e.g. *The NewsHour with Jim Lehrer* (PBS)

3 chat shows: e.g. *Piers Morgan Tonight* (CNN)

4 comedy shows: e.g. *Saturday Night Live* (NBC)

Televised presidential debates

There are the traditional televised presidential debates during the general election campaign. This is what you need to know about these debates:

- They began in 1960, between Kennedy and Nixon, but were not used again until 1976.

- They have been used in every election year since then.

- There are usually three presidential debates and one vice-presidential debate, each lasting 1½ hours.

- They generally include only Democrat and Republican candidates, though Ross Perot and his running-mate James Stockdale were included in 1992.

- Most have been in the format of a joint press conference with a panel of journalists asking questions.

- But from 1992, 'town hall' style debates have also been used — a more informal style with questions put by an invited audience.

These debates can be important. The following rules of thumb for the debaters should be noted:

- Style is often more important than substance — it's not what you say, but how you say it and how you look.

- Avoid serious gaffes.

- Look for opportunities to deliver a 'sound bite' that will be used by the news organisations in their 'highlights'.

- Debates are more difficult for incumbent presidents than for challengers because incumbents have a record to defend and can have their words from 4 years ago quoted back at them.

Television commercials

Television commercials date from the 1952 campaign. They are usually 30-second commercials, but may be longer nearer Election Day.

There are different types of commercial. There are those that are *positive* about your candidate. These may be either biographical or policy orientated. There are also *negative* commercials, talking only about your opponent. These may be either 'attack ads' or humorous — attempting to poke fun at your opponent.

Discussion regarding television commercials centres upon:

- cost

- whether 'attack ads' are double-edged swords, which hurt the purveyor more than the intended target

Now test yourself

22 In which year were the first television debates held?

23 Which was the only year when a third-party candidate was included in the debates?

24 Why are the television debates more difficult for an incumbent president than for a challenger?

25 What are the two important functions of television commercials in the general election campaign?

Tested ☐

- the extent to which commercials change voters' minds and voting intentions
- evidence that commercials do little in the way of **conversion** but more in terms of **reinforcement** and **activation** — reinforcing what voters already think and activating them to turn out and vote for your candidate

Electoral College

We turn now to the final stage of the presidential election, the voting of the **Electoral College**.

How it works

- Each state is awarded a certain number of Electoral College votes (ECVs).
- This number is equal to that state's representation in Congress — the number of Senators (2) plus the number of Representatives. Thus in 2008, California had 55 ECVs while Wyoming had only three.
- There are a total of 538 ECVs.
- To win the presidency, a candidate must win an **absolute majority** of ECVs — that is, 270.
- Whichever candidate wins the most popular votes in a state receives all the ECVs of that state. This is not in the Constitution, but 48 of the 50 states have a state law requiring it.
- The other two states — Maine and Nebraska — award ECVs on a different basis, depending on who wins the presidential vote in each congressional district.
- The Electoral College never meets together. The Electors meet in their respective state capitals on the Monday after the second Wednesday in December and send their results to the vice-president in Washington DC.
- If no candidate wins 270 ECVs, the president would be elected by the House of Representatives, each state having one vote — that is, a total of 50 votes.
- The vice-president would be elected by the Senate, each senator having one vote — that is, a total of 100 votes.
- The winners would need to receive an absolute majority of the votes in the respective chambers.
- Only twice has the Electoral College failed to come up with a winner and the election been thrown to Congress — 1800 and 1824.

> **Electoral College:** the institution established by the Founding Fathers to elect the president.

> **Examiner's tip**
>
> The number of Electoral College votes that each state has is equal to the state's representation in Congress (i.e. the number of senators (2) plus the number of seats in the House of Representatives), but the people who cast the Electoral College votes are not the Senate and House members themselves.

> **Typical mistakes**
>
> Be careful to get this right. An absolute majority is more than everyone else put together: 50% + 1.

> **Examiner's tip**
>
> Don't worry too much about who the Electors actually are. Examiners will not expect you to know that level of detail.

Strengths and weaknesses of the Electoral College system

Strengths of the electoral college system	Weaknesses of the electoral college system
(1) Preserves the voice of the small-population states.	(1) Small-population states over-represented.
(2) Promotes a two-horse race, with the winner therefore likely to receive over 50% of the popular vote, giving the president a mandate to govern. In 25 of the last 37 elections (67%), the winner has gained more than 50% of the popular vote, but not in 1992, 1996 or 2000.	(2) Winner-takes-all system can distort the result: e.g. in 2008 Obama won 52% of the popular vote but 68% of the Electoral College votes. (contd)

Strengths of the electoral college system	Weaknesses of the electoral college system
	(3) Possible for a candidate to win the popular vote but lose in the Electoral College: e.g. Gore in 2000.
	(4) Unfair to national third parties: e.g. Perot in 1992 gained 19% of the popular vote, but no ECVs.
	(5) So-called 'rogue' or 'faithless' Electors vote for candidates other than the one who won the popular vote in their state.
	(6) The system used in the case of an Electoral College deadlock could result in the House choosing a president of one party and the Senate choosing a vice-president of another party.

Debate

Strengths and weaknesses of the Electoral College

Possible reforms of the Electoral College system — Revised

Here are three possible reforms of the Electoral College system:

1 Abandon the winner-takes-all system for a more proportional system (already used by two states — Maine and Nebraska). Had Florida been using a proportional system in 2000, it might have eased the problem. Instead of deciding who was going to get 25 ECVs and who was going to get none, it might instead have decided who should receive 13 ECVs and who should get 12.

2 Pass state laws to prohibit 'rogue' Electors from casting such rogue votes.

3 Abolish the Electoral College altogether and decide the election on the popular vote. The problem with this is that it would encourage a multi-candidate election with the winner gaining maybe only 35–40% of the votes.

Now test yourself

26 How are the Electoral College votes allocated among the 50 states?

27 How many ECVs does a candidate need to win the presidency?

28 How do most states allocate their ECVs?

29 (a) What are the strengths of the Electoral College? (b) What are its weaknesses?

30 What would be the main problem with abolishing the Electoral College altogether?

Tested

Voting behaviour in presidential elections — Revised

The subject of voting behaviour looks at the factors that explain the outcomes of recent presidential elections and answer certain questions about why people vote as they do:

● How important is party affiliation?
● Are there differences in the voting habits of men and women?
● How important is race in voting?
● What about religious groups?
● What about the voting habits of the poor as opposed to the better-off?
● Does geographic region have anything to tell us?
● What role do policies play?

Party affiliation — Revised

Despite all we say about political parties not being all that important in US politics, party affiliation seems to be an important ingredient in determining voting. In the 2008 presidential election:

- 71% of voters identified with one of the two major parties: 39% called themselves Democrats; 32% called themselves Republicans
- 89% of the Democrats voted for Obama
- 90% of the Republicans voted for McCain

In the presidential elections between 1952 and 2008, the party that had the highest level of support from its own identifiers (those identifying with it) won on 12 out of 15 occasions, but 2008 was one of the three occasions when this was not the case. Winning elections is as much about mobilising your own supporters as it is about converting supporters of your opponent so that they vote for you. It is also about who manages to get people to the voting booths on Election Day. Do your supporters turn out or stay at home? Elections are determined just as much by the stay-at-homes as by those who turn up to vote.

Gender

With regards to gender and voting, the following points are worth noting:

- Women are more likely to be registered voters than men.
- Women tend to turn out in higher numbers on Election Day than men.
- In recent elections, the trend has been for men to be more supportive of Republican candidates while women have tended to support the Democrats. (But in 2008, men split 49–48 for Obama–McCain.) This is what is called the **gender gap**.
- In the presidential elections between 1964 and 2008, women were more supportive than men of the Democrats in 11 out of 12 elections. (In 2008, women voted 56–43 for Obama–McCain.)
- Women are more likely to be registered Democrats than registered Republicans.

The reasons for this gender gap are thought to derive from the stance of the two major parties on such policies as:

- abortion — Democrats tend to be 'pro-choice' and Republicans tend to be 'pro-life'
- defence — women tend to favour lower levels of spending on defence: the Democrats' position
- law and order — women tend to oppose capital punishment: again the Democrats' position
- gun control — women tend to support this; another Democrat position
- women's rights — Democrats supported the Equal Rights Amendment; Republicans tended to oppose it.

So, to win elections, the Republicans are always looking for ways to appeal more to women voters, while Democrats are trying to attract more male voters. And because there are more women than men among registered voters, the larger the turnout, the better it is for the Democrats.

Race

African-Americans

African-Americans, who make up some 10% of the US electorate, have since the 1960s given solid support to the Democratic Party. Traditionally,

The **gender gap** is the gap between the support given to a candidate by women and the support given to the same candidate by men.

Typical mistakes

When writing about voting behaviour, it is easy carelessly to state, or even to suggest, that 'women' vote this way, or 'southerners' vote that way, as if everyone in the group votes alike. While the majority of women tend to support Democrat candidates, many women, of course, vote Republican.

the Republicans — 'the party of Lincoln' — had thought of the black vote as theirs, following Lincoln's freeing of the slaves after the Civil War. But that changed during the twentieth century for two reasons. First, it was Democrat Franklin Roosevelt's 'New Deal' that helped out-of-work and poor African-Americans in the 1930s. Secondly, Democrats Kennedy and Johnson got Congress to pass civil rights laws that protected the rights of African-Americans in such matters as housing, education, employment and voting. In the eight presidential elections between 1980 and 2008, African-Americans never gave less than 83% support to the Democrat candidate. In 2008, it was 95%.

Hispanics

Hispanics are a more diverse group and encompass:

- Cuban-Americans
- Mexican-Americans
- Puerto Rican-Americans
- those from other Central American countries

But they are a numerically growing group. Hence their importance increases at each election.

Cuban-Americans, especially those in South Florida, have tended to support Republican candidates. Other Hispanic groups, such as those in California and New Mexico, have tended to support Democrats.

In the 2000 and 2004 elections, the Republicans were seen courting the Hispanic vote. In 1996, only 20% of Hispanic voters voted for Republican Bob Dole. By 2004, 43% of them voted for George W. Bush, but this fell back to just 31% for John McCain in 2008.

Religion

There are certain trends in voting according to religion, a factor much stronger in US politics than in the UK. Note the following four points:

1 Protestant voters tend to vote Republican. They did not give Clinton a majority of their votes in either 1992 or 1996 — they went for George H. W. Bush in 1992 (45–34%) and for Dole in 1996 (47–43%). They broke in favour of George W. Bush in 2004 (59–40%) and in favour of McCain in 2008 (54%–45%).

2 Catholic voters tend to vote Democrat, though not as strongly as used to be the case. But they did give Clinton a 54–37% vote in 1992 and 42–37% in 1996. The Democrats' pro-choice position on abortion can be a liability with Catholic voters. But in 2004, Bush won the majority of Catholic voters: 52–47%. In 2008, Obama won 54% of Catholic voters with just 45% going for McCain.

3 Jewish voters tend to vote Democrat pretty solidly. They gave Clinton 78% support in both 1992 and 1996. They have given a majority of their votes to the Democrat candidate in every presidential election since the Second World War. In 2000, they gave 79% support to the Gore–Lieberman ticket. So Al Gore's choice of Joseph Lieberman — an orthodox Jew — as his running-mate in 2000 did not obviously help him politically with Jews.

4 In the 2000 presidential election, there was a high correlation between attendance at religious services and voting Republican. Of those voters

Typical mistakes

It is easy to exaggerate the importance of the Jewish vote. Remember, they constitute a mere 3% of the electorate, so are nowhere near as important as Protestant or Catholic voters as a bloc.

who attend religious services weekly or more than weekly — and that was 42% of all voters — 63% voted for George W. Bush, but this correlation was much less clear in 2008.

Wealth

There is a strong correlation between relative wealth and likely support of the two major parties. In both 1992 and 1996, Clinton had his highest support among those earning under $15,000 (£10,000) a year and his lowest support among those earning over $100,000 (£66,000) a year. Likewise, in both elections, the Republicans received their lowest support among the poorest and their highest support among the wealthiest. The pattern was repeated in 2004, with Kerry winning 63% of the poorest voters but only 41% of the wealthiest, while Bush won only 36% of the poorest voters but 58% of the wealthiest. In 2008, Obama won a majority among both the very poor (73%) and the very rich (52%).

Geographic region

There are certain trends in voting according to geographic region. Consider the following four points:

1 The Northeast tends to support the Democrats. The region's big cities gave Bill Clinton his highest level of support in any region in both 1992 and 1996, and likewise for Gore in 2000, Kerry in 2004 and Obama in 2008. This is bad news for the Democrats — demographically, the Northeast is a declining region. Fewer people mean less political clout.

2 From the end of the Civil War in the 1860s until the 1960s, the South was described as 'the solid South' — voting solidly for the Democratic Party. But in the last three decades of the twentieth century, the 'solid South' for the Democrats has collapsed. The South voted for George H. W. Bush in 1992, Bob Dole in 1996, George W. Bush in 2000 and 2004, and John McCain in 2008. In 2008, the South was the only region to vote Republican. Strength in the South is good news for the Republicans — demographically, the South is a growing region. More people mean more political clout.

3 The West tends to support the Democrats. States such as California, Oregon and Washington voted solidly for Clinton in 1992 and 1996, although Green Party candidate Ralph Nader nibbled away at Gore's majority in the Pacific Northwest in 2000. Kerry won all three west coast states in 2004, as did Obama in 2008.

4 The Midwest is the battleground in modern elections. In 2000, the Midwest broke 49–48% between Bush and Gore. Nationally it was 48–48%. In 2004, the Midwest broke 51–48% between Bush and Kerry, exactly the same as the national vote. And in 2008, Obama won the Midwest 54–44%, similar to the national vote. Today's presidential elections are largely won and lost in Missouri, Michigan and Ohio. In all 12 presidential elections between 1960 and 2004, whoever won Missouri won the White House. This was not the case in 2008, with McCain winning the state by just one percentage point. But Obama did win Michigan and Ohio. Ohio has now voted for the winner in every presidential election since 1964.

Policies

Revised

Policies matter, but which ones? They can easily change from one election to another. Here are five important points to note about policies and voting:

1 In the 1992 election, a Clinton campaign sign said that it was 'the economy, stupid!' In that election, voters who thought the economy was in 'good shape' voted 82% for George H. W. Bush, while those who thought it in 'poor shape' voted 65% for Bill Clinton. The trouble for Bush was that twice as many voters fell into the second category as into the first.

2 In 1992, Bush also suffered from the fact that in an election in which he was trumpeting his foreign policy successes — most notably, victory in the Persian Gulf War — only 8% of voters thought that foreign policy mattered as an issue. That figure had been 23% back in 1988 when Bush was elected.

3 In 2000, the four issues most frequently mentioned by voters as being those that mattered were: the economy and jobs; education; social security; taxes. But voters preferred Al Gore's position on the first three. Only on taxes did George W. Bush have a majority who preferred his policies — but it was 80–17%!

4 In 2004, the four main issues were 'moral values', the economy/jobs, terrorism and Iraq. When 2004 voters were asked which issue mattered most in deciding their vote, 22% said 'moral values', 20% said the economy and jobs, 19% said terrorism and 15% the war in Iraq.

5 In 2008, 63% of voters in exit polls said that the economy was the most important issue, with the second most important issue — the war in Iraq — being named by only 10% of voters. Among the 63% of voters who identified the economy as the most important issue, Obama beat McCain by 53% to 44%, almost the same as the nationwide popular vote.

Typical voters

Revised

● The old Democrat '**New Deal coalition**' has weakened. (This refers to a coalition including urban workers, racial minorities, farmers, southerners and liberals.)

● During the 1990s, Bill Clinton tried to move the Democratic Party away from its old 'tax and spend', liberal base to a more centrist 'third way'.

● The Democrats have lost significant support among Southern whites and have a problem attracting male voters, but they are still strong in the Northeast.

● The Republicans have experienced difficulties attracting women voters and those of racial minorities, but they are strong among white, evangelical Christians and in the so-called 'sun-belt' states.

● Typical Democrat voting blocs: blue-collar, unionised workers; urban dwellers; West and Northeast; Catholic; Jewish; racial minority, possibly black or Hispanic; female; liberal; less wealthy; less well educated.

● Typical Republican voting blocs: white-collar, professional workers; suburban and rural; sun-belt; Protestant, especially evangelical; white; male; conservative; wealthy; college-educated.

Now test yourself

31 What do the last 15 elections tell us about the importance of party in voting?

32 What policies tend to attract more women voters to the Democrats than the Republicans?

33 Why do African-Americans vote overwhelmingly for Democratic candidates?

34 What patterns of voting are found among Protestant and Catholic voters?

35 What has happened to voting trends in the South over the past 50 years?

36 Which region is now the battle-ground region for presidential elections?

37 What policy issue dominated the 2008 election?

38 How do typical Democrat and typical Republican voters differ?

Congressional elections

Overview

Congressional elections:

- occur every 2 years when the whole of the House of Representatives and one-third of the Senate are elected
- either coincide with the presidential election (in years divisible by 4, i.e. 2004, 2008, 2012 etc.) or occur midway through the presidential term (called **mid-term elections** — in 2006, 2010, 2014 etc.)

Article I of the Constitution states that to be eligible to be a member of Congress, one must fulfil certain requirements regarding age, citizenship and residency. To be a member of the House of Representatives, one must:

- be at least 25 years of age
- have been a US citizen for at least 7 years
- be a resident of the state your **congressional district** is in

Some states have a **locality rule** which means that House members must be residents of the district they represent.

To be a member of the Senate, one must:

- be at least 30 years of age
- have been a US citizen for at least 9 years
- be a resident of the state you represent

> **Congressional elections** are elections held every 2 years for the whole of the House of Representatives and one-third of the Senate.
>
> **Mid-term elections** are the elections for the whole of the House of Representatives and one-third of the Senate that occur midway through the president's 4-year term of office.
>
> A **congressional district** is a geographic division of a state from which a member of the House of Representatives is elected.
>
> The **locality rule** is a state law that requires members of the House of Representatives to be resident within the congressional district they represent.

Now test yourself

39 What parts of Congress are elected every 2 years?

40 What are mid-term elections?

41 How do the qualifications for the House differ from those for the Senate?

42 What is a congressional district?

43 What is the locality rule?

Trends in congressional elections

Primaries

Candidates for congressional elections must first secure the nomination of their party. As virtually all 535 members of Congress are either Democrats or Republicans, this means securing the nomination of one of the two major parties through the Democratic or Republican congressional primary. Sometimes, even an incumbent House member or senator might be challenged for the nomination in the upcoming election and will therefore have to enter the primary. Defeat for incumbents in the primary is unusual. Between 1982 and 2010 — 15 election cycles — only 66 House members and seven senators were defeated in congressional primaries. Three of those senate primary defeats occurred in 2010.

Examiner's tip

To avoid confusion, use the term 'House members' to refer to members of the House of Representatives.

Coat-tails effect

The **coat-tails effect** is the effect of a strong candidate for a party at the top of the ticket (i.e. president, state governor) helping congressional candidates of the same party to get elected at the same time. The coat-tails effect had not been evident in elections for over two decades. In 1980, the Republican presidential candidate Ronald Reagan helped the Republicans gain 33 seats in the House and 12 seats in the Senate. But in 2008, Democrat presidential candidate Barack Obama helped the Democrats gain 21 seats in the House and eight seats in the Senate, leading some commentators to say that Obama was the first president since Reagan to have genuine coat-tails.

Split-ticket voting

Split-ticket voting is the practice of voting for candidates of two or more parties for different offices at the same election. The opposite — voting for candidates of the same party for different offices at the same election — is called **straight-ticket voting**. In 2008, just 83 congressional districts (19% of the total) voted differently in the presidential and House elections. In 34 districts, Obama won the presidential race but the Republican won the House race; 49 districts voted McCain for president but Democrat in the House race.

Split-ticket voting in congressional elections which coincide with the presidential election may result in **divided government** — one party controlling the White House, while the other party controls the two houses of Congress. This occurred in 1996, when voters re-elected Democrat president Bill Clinton but also elected Republican majorities to both the House and the Senate. In the 40 years between 1969 and 2009, the USA had divided government for 22 years, including the last 6 years of Bill Clinton's presidency (1995–2001) and the last 2 years of George W. Bush's presidency (2007–09).

The power of incumbency

An **incumbent** is the House member or senator who currently holds the seat. Congressional elections show high levels of support for incumbents, or put another way, there are high rates of re-election in congressional elections. In the House, re-election rates have exceeded 90% in nine of the last 11 congressional elections, though 2010 was one of the two elections when this did not occur. In the same period

(1990–2010), re-election rates in the Senate ranged from a high of 96% in 2004 to a low of 79% in 2006.

Decline in competitive races in House elections

Between 1992 and 2004, there was a significant trend towards fewer genuinely competitive seats in elections to the House of Representatives. A competitive seat is one that was won by the incumbent by less than 10 percentage points. In 1992, there were 111 such seats in the House. By 2004, the figure had fallen to just 31. In other words, following the 2004 congressional elections, 404 out of the 435 House members — or just less than 93% — were in what we would call safe seats. But the 2006, 2008 and 2010 congressional elections have seen increases in the numbers of competitive House races.

There are two important consequences when House seats become uncompetitive. First, incumbents in safe seats tend to vote in the House in a way that pleases only those voters from their own party. This leads to an increase in **partisanship** and a decrease in compromise and cross-party cooperation. Secondly, House members in safe seats have more to fear from an intra-party challenge in a primary than from an inter-party challenge in the general election. Hence the primary becomes the real political battleground and winning the primary is tantamount to winning re-election.

The president's party tends to lose seats in mid-term elections

The mid-term elections are those that occur midway through a president's term, such as those held in 2010. In the 96-year period since the Senate was first directly elected (1914–2010), the president's party has lost an average of 30 seats in the House and just four seats in the Senate in mid-term elections. In 2010, President Obama's Democratic Party lost 63 House seats and six Senate seats. During this 96-year period, on only two occasions — 1934 and 2002 — has the president's party gained seats in both houses in the mid-term elections. In 2002, Bush's Republicans gained five House seats and two Senate seats, largely as a result of the events of 11 September 2001 (9/11) and Bush's 'war on terror'.

> **Typical mistakes**
>
> It is easy to give the impression that partisanship is, in itself, a bad thing. But parties standing up for and sticking to what they believe in is not necessarily always bad. Indeed, some voters will want them to do just that!

> **Partisanship** denotes a situation in which members of one party regularly group together in opposition to members of another party.

> **Now test yourself**
>
> 44 What is the coat-tails effect?
> 45 What is split-ticket voting?
> 46 How high have the rates of re-election been in recent House and Senate elections?
> 47 What tends to happen to the president's party in mid-term elections?
>
> Tested ☐

Propositions, referendums and recall elections

Propositions ———————————————————————— Revised ☐

A **proposition**, more commonly referred to as an initiative in the USA, is provided for in 24 states.

There are two types of proposition:

- Direct propositions: proposals that qualify go directly on the ballot.
- Indirect propositions: proposals are submitted to the state legislature, which decides on further action.

> A **proposition** is a mechanism by which citizens of a state can place proposed laws, and in some states proposed constitutional amendments, on the state ballot.

Exam practice answers and quick quizzes at **www.therevisionbutton.co.uk/myrevisionnotes**

There are a few general rules of thumb regarding getting propositions on the state ballot paper. A proposed proposition must be:

- filed with a designated state official
- reviewed for conformance with state legal requirements
- given a formal title and brief summary for inclusion on the ballot paper
- circulated to gain the required number of signatures from registered voters
- submitted to state officials for verification of signatures

Recent examples of state propositions are:

- a ban on same-sex marriage approved in seven states including Virginia in 2006 and California in 2008
- an increase in the state minimum wage level approved in six states including Missouri and Montana in 2006

Advantages of propositions are as follows:

- They provide a way of enacting reforms on controversial issues that state legislatures are often unwilling or unable to act upon.
- They increase the responsiveness and accountability of state legislatures.
- They can help increase voter turnout.
- They increase citizen interest in state issues and may also encourage pressure group membership.

Disadvantages of propositions are:

- They lack the flexibility of the legislative process.
- They are vulnerable to manipulation by special interests.

Debate

Advantages and disadvantages of propositions

Referendums

Revised

A **referendum** is an electoral device, available in all 50 states, by which voters can effectively veto a bill passed by the state legislature. A number of states require that changes to the state constitution must be approved by a state-wide referendum. In other states, changes in state tax must be approved in this way.

In 24 states there is provision for a popular referendum. In these states, such as Alaska and New Mexico, if the state legislature passes a law that voters do not approve of, they may gather signatures to demand a referendum on the law. Usually there is a 90-day period after the law is passed during which the petitioning must take place. If voters reject the law in the ensuing referendum, the law is null and void — a kind of popular veto.

Recall elections

Revised

A **recall election** is a procedure that enables voters in a state to remove an elected official from office before their term has expired — a kind of direct form of **impeachment** (see p. 66). There are 19 states that make provision for recall elections. The most recent and high-profile recall election was of California's Democrat governor Gray Davis in 2003 and the subsequent election of Republican Arnold Schwarzenegger.

Now test yourself

48 What is a proposition?

49 How many states provide for propositions?

50 Distinguish between a direct and an indirect proposition.

51 Give two recent examples of propositions.

52 What are (a) the advantages and (b) the disadvantages of propositions?

53 What is a referendum?

54 What is a recall election?

Answers on p. 107–108

Exam practice

A Short answer questions:

    1 What's wrong with the system of presidential candidate selection? [15]

    2 What important functions are performed by the National Party Conventions? [15]

    3 Analyse the strengths and weaknesses of the Electoral College. [15]

    4 Explain the advantages and disadvantages of the states' use of propositions. [15]

B Essay questions:

    1 What does anyone need to become president of the United States? [45]

    2 Why do presidential elections last so long? [45]

    3 Discuss the main factors that determine how people vote in presidential elections. [45]

    4 Why are mid-term elections potentially important? [45]

Answers and quick quiz 1 online

Online

2 Political parties

Organisation of the two major parties

National organisation

Revised

The USA has a federal system of government (see pp. 56–60). **Federalism** is a decentralised form of government. Some powers are vested in the national government, but other equally important powers are vested in the state governments. The more centralised the government, the more centralised the party system. The less centralised the government, the less centralised the party system. Thus, US political parties are **decentralised**. Certainly there is some national organisation, but it does not amount to much. US political parties are principally state-based.

The two major US parties — the Democrats and the Republicans — do have something of a national party organisation, but it is fairly limited. Each has a **National Committee**. The Democratic National Committee (DNC) and the Republican National Committee (RNC) are each headed by a **party chairman**. He or she acts as a spokesperson for the national party, especially in the media, and is responsible for the day-to-day running of the party. Although the DNC and RNC meet in full session only twice a year, they are permanent organisations with offices in Washington DC. And, of course, each party holds a **National Convention** once every 4 years (see pp. 12–14). But that is about it.

> **Examiner's tip**
>
> In the USA, the Republican Party is often referred to as the GOP — the 'Grand Old Party'.

State organisation

Revised

Everything else is done at the state or local level. At that level, the organisation of each party looks something like this:

- State Party Convention
- State Party Committee (headed by the state party chairman)
- County Committees
- District Committees
- City Committees
- Ward Committees
- Precinct Committees

So it is worth noting that US political parties really have no one who can truly be called the 'party leader'. The president might be said to be 'the leader' of the party. But even that does not mean much. The party not in control of the White House does not even have that level of national leadership. Except for the period — once every 4 years — between the National Party Convention and the holding of the presidential election, when both parties do have someone who maybe looks and sounds like a national leader, US national political parties are pretty leaderless. Parties have leaders in Congress — speaker of the House, majority and minority leaders in each chamber, and so on — but their power, such as it is, rarely extends beyond Capitol Hill.

The power of the state parties can be seen at election time in the process of selecting candidates for elections to Congress. Take, for example, the Republicans' nomination for the open Senate seat in Delaware in 2010. The national party's preferred candidate was Congressman — and former state governor — Mike Castle, a moderate Republican. But he lost in the state Republican primary to Christine O'Donnell, a Tea Party-backed conservative. It is the state party that invariably holds the upper hand. Power in the parties rests at state level, not national level.

> **Examiner's tip**
>
> In essays, you can make an interesting comparison with the very different situation in UK political parties.

Now test yourself

Tested ☐

1 What is the main reason why US political parties are decentralised?
2 What organisation do the Democrats and Republicans have at the national level?
3 How can the power of state parties be seen at election time?

Traditions and ideologies

Traditions of the two major parties

Revised ☐

Both of today's major parties are rooted in history and tradition, shaped by the big issues of American history. Here are six big issues that have helped to shape the Democratic and Republican parties into what they are today:

1 *The form of government.* Back in the 1780s, the Federalists (the forerunners of the Republicans), who represented the commercial and business interests, favoured a more centralised form of government; the Anti-Federalists (the forerunners of the Democrats), who represented the agricultural and land-owning interests, favoured a more decentralised form of government.

2 *Democracy.* Another major issue at this time was the level of democracy to be written into the workings of government. In 1828, Andrew Jackson renamed the Democratic-Republicans (formerly the Anti-Federalists) the Democratic Party. Jackson was committed to expanding direct democracy and serving the interests of the poor, immigrants and minority groups.

3 *Slavery.* By 1860, the Democrats had become the party of the South, preaching the economic virtues of slavery. They lost the Civil War and became the party of small farmers, urban workers, immigrants and Catholics and, for the next 100 years, the party of the (Solid) South. The new Republican Party under Lincoln became the party of the North, opposing slavery, winning the Civil War and continuing as the party of big business, industrialists, free enterprise and the Protestant work ethic.

4 *The economy.* The great depression of the 1930s did for the Republicans what the Civil War had done for the Democrats

> **Examiner's tip**
>
> But in essays, don't spend too much time going back to the 1780s, or even the 1930s.

Exam practice answers and quick quizzes at **www.therevisionbutton.co.uk/myrevisionnotes**

70 years earlier — sent them into the political wilderness for a generation and more. The Democrats, meanwhile, put together the New Deal Coalition of southern white conservatives and northeastern liberals, of city dwellers, blue-collar workers, Catholics, Jews and ethnic minorities. The Republicans gained such support as they had from the Midwest and Plains States, WASPS (white, Anglo-Saxon Protestants) and white-collar workers.

5 *Civil rights.* From the 1950s onwards, the Democrats became more and more associated with favouring the promotion of civil rights for racial minorities through affirmative action programmes as well as using all the resources of the federal government to support the rights of the disadvantaged. It was this support that eventually brought an end to the Solid (Democratic) South (see p. 32) after more than a century and splintered the New Deal Coalition.

6 *The role of the federal government.* By the 1930s, the two parties had both reversed their earlier positions: Republicans favouring decentralised government and Democrats favouring centralised government. The role of the federal government and the relationship between it and the state governments has continued as a traditional determining issue for both parties: the Democrats favouring federal government power; the Republicans stressing decentralisation and states' rights.

Ideology of the two major parties   Revised

In terms of ideology, both major parties in the USA have traditionally been seen as quite diverse, causing considerable conflicts and tensions within them.

- The Democratic Party is usually associated with being **liberal**.
- The Republican Party is normally thought of as being **conservative**.
- Yet Democrats traditionally came in many shades — 'liberal Democrats', 'moderate Democrats', 'New Democrats' and even still a few 'conservative Democrats'.
- Likewise, there were 'moderate Republicans', 'conservative Republicans', 'Christian conservatives' and 'compassionate conservatives'.
- The key to understanding much of this is geography.
- In the Northeast — in states like New York, Massachusetts and Maine — one would tend to find 'liberal Democrats' and 'moderate Republicans'; the same was true on the west coast — in states like California.
- But in the South you would tend to come across 'conservative Democrats' and 'conservative Republicans'.
- Both parties took on different ideological colours from region to region; if they had not, they would not have been national parties.
- In the 1960s, the Democratic Party contained both 'liberal Democrats' like John F. Kennedy, pushing for civil rights for African-Americans, and 'conservative Democrats' like Governor George Wallace of Alabama, whom many would have regarded as an unreformed racist.
- At the same time, the Republican Party contained both 'conservative Republicans' like Senator Barry Goldwater and 'liberal Republicans' like Governor Nelson Rockefeller of New York.

Liberal is a view that seeks to change the political, economic and social status quo in favour of the well-being, rights and liberties of the individual, and especially those who are generally disadvantaged.

Conservative is a view that seeks to defend the political, economic and social status quo and therefore tends to oppose changes in the institutions and structures of society.

Typical mistakes

Be careful: they are 'conservatives' (relating to a conservative ideology) not 'Conservatives' (members of a Conservative Party).

- It seemed as if both parties contained people from right across the left–right ideological spectrum.
- But the parties today are much less diverse than used to be the case back then.
- Democrats have lost most of their conservatives to the Republicans or to retirement or defeat at election time.
- Meanwhile, moderate Republicans have likewise largely disappeared.

Increasing partisanship

Revised

There was a time was when the southern states were referred to as the **'Solid South'.** This is because voters in the South voted solidly for the Democratic Party. This was a consequence of the Civil War, fought in the 1860s. During the Civil War, the Republicans were thought of as the party of the North, the Democrats as the party of the South. And for a century and more, people in the South would use the slogan 'vote as you shot'.

From 1960 to 1990, a slow breakdown occurred in the Solid South. In 1960:

- House members from the South comprised 99 Democrats and just 7 Republicans.
- All 22 Senators from the South were Democrats.
- All 11 state governors in the South were Democrats.

By 1992, the Democrats still had a majority in each of these three groups, but a much reduced one. Table 2.1 shows what has happened in the last 20 years — a dramatic collapse of support for Democrats in the South. The result has been to:

- widen the differences between the two major parties and lessen the differences within them
- cause both parties to become more ideologically cohesive
- increase partisanship in Congress

Table 2.1 Final break-up of the 'Solid South', 1992–2010

Year	House: Democrats–Republicans	Senate: Democrats–Republicans	Governors: Democrats–Republicans
1992	77–48	13–9	8–3
1994	61–64	9–13	5–6
1996	54–71	7–15	5–6
1998	54–71	8–14	4–7
2000	53–71	9–13	5–6
2002	55–76	9–13	4–7
2004	49–82	4–18	4–7
2006	54–77	5–17	5–6
2008	59–72	7–15	4–7
2010	38–94	6–16	2–9

As US politics moved into the twenty-first century, pundits started to talk about the USA as a **'50–50 nation'**, split in half between **red America** (voting Republican) and **blue America** (voting Democrat). The colours are those used by the media on electoral maps. This was most plainly seen in the 2000 elections, in which both parties ended up with around 49% of the popular vote, the Electoral College vote split 271–267, the House of Representatives was 221–212 with two independents, while the Senate split exactly 50–50.

Typical mistakes

Be careful not to suggest that 'everyone' living in Red America is one thing, and 'everyone' living in Blue America is the opposite. There are plenty of Republicans in blue states and many Democrats in red states.

Table 2.2 Differences between red and blue America

Red (Republican) America is portrayed as:	Blue (Democrat) America is portrayed as:
More male than female	More female than male
Overwhelmingly white	A rainbow coalition of white, black, Hispanic and Asian
Protestant and, specifically, born-again evangelical	Catholic, but not especially church-going
Wealthy	Less wealthy
Rural (and maybe suburban)	Predominantly urban
Southern or Midwestern	Northeastern, Great Lakes or west coast
Conservative	Liberal

Commentators also noticed increased **partisanship** in US politics — be it in voting behaviour among the electorate, or the tone of debate and voting in Congress. A number of factors were said to have contributed towards this increase in partisanship:

Partisanship denotes a situation in which members of one party regularly group together in opposition to members of another party.

- the shift of southern conservative Democrats to the Republican Party
- the end of the Cold War consensus in foreign policy following the demise of the Soviet Union
- the polarising presidencies of Bill Clinton, George W. Bush and Barack Obama
- the effect of the 'new media' such as direct mail, talk radio, cable television and the internet

Now test yourself

Tested ☐

4   Name the three most recent issues that have helped to shape the two major parties.
5   Explain the term 'liberal'.
6   Explain the term 'conservative'.
7   Which party most follows each of these two ideologies?
8   What did the term 'Solid South' refer to?
9   What has happened to the Solid South in the last 20 years?
10 Explain the terms (a) red America and (b) blue America.
11 What are the main characteristics of (a) red America and (b) blue America?
12 Give two reasons for increased partisanship in US politics.

The two-party system

Revised ☐

The facts

That the USA does have a **two-party system** is almost indisputable. Look at the following facts:

- Every president since 1856 has been either a Democrat or a Republican.
- In every presidential election since 1916, the combined Democrat and Republican vote has exceeded 80% of the total votes cast.
- In 21 of those last 25 presidential elections, the combined Democrat and Republican vote has exceeded 90% of the total votes cast, reaching 99% in both 1984 and 1988.
- In January 2011, every member of the US Senate belonged to one of the two major parties, except Senator Bernie Sanders of Vermont, who sits as an Independent, and Senator Joe Lieberman, an Independent Democrat.
- At the same time, all of the 435 members of the House of Representatives are either Democrats or Republicans.
- Of the 50 state governors, 49 were either Democrats or Republicans and the one Independent governor — Lincoln Chafee of Rhode Island — is a former Republican senator.

> A **two-party system** is a party system in which two major parties regularly win the vast majority of votes in general elections, regularly capture nearly all of the seats in the legislature, and alternately control the executive branch of government.

The reasons

Revised ☐

There are two main reasons why the USA has a two-party system:

1 the first-past-the-post, winner-takes-all electoral system

2 the all-embracing nature of the two major parties, which allows little room for third parties

But it could be argued that the USA does *not* have a two-party system, or that at least the picture is rather more complex than the statistics above would lead us to believe. Consider other analyses of the US party system.

Other analyses

Revised ☐

Some commentators have suggested that the USA does not have a two-party system but a **50-party system**. Each individual state has its own party system.

Another analysis suggests that some states appear to have a **one-party system**. In such states, one party dominates to such an extent that the other seems hardly to exist. For example, the Democratic Party dominates Massachusetts. The Republicans have won the state in only one presidential election in the last 50 years, Reagan winning it by just 3,000 votes out of 2½ million in 1980. In Wyoming, it is the Republicans who, in that same period, have won all bar one presidential election (1964) and dominate the state at all levels.

Yet another analysis suggests that, because of the decline in the importance of political parties, the USA might be said to have a **no-party system**. Let us consider this a little more closely.

> **Examiner's tip**
>
> To help you with questions that ask you for arguments for and against the claim that the USA has a two-party system, construct a two-column table, putting arguments for on one side and arguments against on the other.

Now test yourself

Tested

13 What is a two-party system?
14 Give two reasons why the USA has a two-party system.
15 What other analyses are made of the US party system?

The changing significance of parties

Theories of party decline

Revised

It was the late David Broder who popularised the idea of **party decline** in the USA. In the 1970s, he published a book with the title *The Party's Over*. Broder and others have put forward a number of reasons for concluding that the USA's parties were in serious decline:

● Parties have lost control over presidential candidate selection. With the rise in importance of presidential primaries, parties no longer choose the candidates. This is now done by voters in the primaries.

● Parties have been bypassed by federal 'matching funds' in presidential elections. The matching funds — introduced in the mid-1970s — are given to the candidates, not the parties.

● Television, opinion polls and 'new media' have bypassed parties as the medium by which candidates communicate with voters. Party rallies and party-organised 'torch-light' processions etc. were the traditional way in which candidates spoke to and heard from voters. The party was therefore the most important vehicle of communication between politicians and voters. Nowadays, politicians increasingly talk to voters through the media of television and the internet, and voters 'talk back' through opinion polls.

● Campaigns are more candidate-centred and issue-centred than they were. Voters tend to vote more for a particular candidate, or because a candidate holds a certain view on an issue of importance to the voter (e.g. abortion, the environment), than for the party label. This has also shown itself in the rise of **split-ticket voting** (voting for candidates of different parties for different offices at the same election) and of 'independent' voters.

> **Party decline** refers to the theory, popular in the last three decades of the twentieth century, that political parties were in decline in terms of membership, functions and importance.

Debate

Party decline versus party renewal

Theories of party renewal

Revised

More recently, however, many commentators have been arguing that American political parties are undergoing renewal. What are the pointers to the theories of **party renewal**?

● The party decline theories are somewhat exaggerated. When all is said and done, it is still true that all the presidents elected in the twentieth century were either Democrats or Republicans; virtually all members of Congress are either Democrats or Republicans; so too are the vast majority of state governors.

● The parties have fought to regain some control over the presidential candidate selection process. The Democratic Party introduced **super**

> **Party renewal** is the theory that suggests that parties, far from being in decline, are increasingly important in elections, fundraising and organisation, and in Congress.

delegates at their 1984 National Convention. These are professional, elected politicians who are given a vote at the Convention *ex officio*. By 2008, these super delegates accounted for almost 20% of the delegate votes at the Democratic National Convention. In that year Democratic Party super delegates played a major role in the choice of Barack Obama over Hillary Clinton in the presidential nomination race.

- Both parties have made significant strides in modernising their national party structures and network. For the Republicans, the **Brock Reforms** significantly strengthened the standing of the Republican National Committee from the 1980s. And in the 1990s, Democratic National Committee chairman Charles Manatt did much the same for the Democrats, developing computerised direct mail facilities and a permanent headquarters in Washington DC.

- 'Soft money' developed in the 1980s and 1990s. In an attempt to overcome the negative effects of 'matching funds' going directly to candidates rather than the parties, both major parties during the 1980s and 1990s took to raising large sums of 'soft money' which was entirely unregulated and led to new abuses. 'Soft money' was eventually banned by the Campaign Finance Reform Act (2002) — see pp. 15–16.

- There have been moves towards the 'nationalising' of campaigns. Not only has this been seen increasingly in presidential elections, but also it was seen dramatically in the 1994 mid-term congressional elections when the Republican Party launched its **Contract with America**. In 2006, the Democrats had a national policy agenda for that year's mid-term elections entitled 'Six for 06' which accompanied their retaking control of both houses of Congress after 12 years in the minority.

- There is now much evidence of increased levels of partisanship in Congress. By 1995, 'party votes' in Congress reached 73% in the House of Representatives, the highest figure since 1910. In the Senate the same year, 69% of votes were 'party votes', the highest since 1922. This came to a crescendo during the impeachment and trial of President Clinton in 1998 and early 1999. Partisanship continued during the presidency of George W. Bush, especially over issues such as the war in Iraq, stem cell research and the State Children's Health Insurance Program (SCHIP). Not a single Republican voted for President Obama's healthcare reform legislation in 2010 (see also p. 59).

Examiner's tip

To help you with questions that ask you for arguments for and against the claim that US parties are/are not in decline, construct a two-column table, putting arguments for decline on one side and arguments for renewal on the other.

Now test yourself

16 What is meant by the term 'party decline'?
17 What is meant by the term 'party renewal'?

Third parties

Types of third party

There are a number of different types of third party in the USA:

- national (e.g. Reform Party, Green Party, Libertarian Party, Natural Law Party)

- regional (e.g. George Wallace's American Independent Party — 1968)
- state (e.g. New York Conservative Party)
- permanent (e.g. Green Party, Libertarian Party)
- temporary (e.g. American Independent Party, Reform Party)
- issue based (e.g. Green Party)
- ideological (e.g. Socialist Party, Constitution Party)

Here are a few details to give you an idea of what some of these third parties stand for:

- *Constitution Party:* founded as the US Taxpayers' Party in 1992 and renamed in 1999, it is a collection of formerly separate right-wing independent parties and is strongly anti-gun control, anti-tax, anti-immigration, protectionist, anti-United Nations, anti-gay rights, pro-school prayer and 'pro-life'.
- *Green Party:* the informal US affiliate of the European Greens, ideologically on the left of US politics.
- *Libertarian Party:* stands for total individual liberty and is pro-drug legalisation, 'pro-choice', pro-gay marriage, pro-home schooling and anti-gun control. It also stands for total economic freedom.

What the USA does not have are national, permanent third parties that regularly win at least 5% of the popular vote in general elections. US third parties are either national and permanent but insignificant (such as the Libertarian Party), or not national and permanent. Even Ross Perot's Reform Party, after impressive nationwide performances in 1992 and 1996, disintegrated in 2000. The most successful third-party candidate in the 2008 presidential election was Ralph Nader, who gained just 0.32% of the popular vote.

Typical mistakes

Avoid giving the impression that anyone standing for or voting for a minor party is an 'extremist'. There are 'extremists' in US politics, but there are many sound and sensible reasons for voting for or standing for a third party.

Examiner's tip

Examiners have sometimes asked candidates to debate the claim that there are 'no third parties' in the USA. To answer this, you would need to state clearly what is meant by a third party.

Impact of third parties

Revised

In recent presidential elections, third parties have enjoyed limited success. The last third-party candidate to gain more than 5% of the popular vote was Ross Perot for the Reform Party in 1996. The last third-party candidate to gain any Electoral College votes was George Wallace with 46 in 1968.

Third parties have also had limited representation in Congress, as is shown in Table 2.3. As of January 2011, 433 of the 435 members of Congress were either Democrats or Republicans — all except senators Bernie Sanders of Vermont and Joe Lieberman of Connecticut, and Senator Lieberman had already announced his intention to retire by the end of 2012.

Table 2.3 Third-party members of Congress since 1990

Years	House/Senate	Name	Party	State
1993–	House/Senate	Bernie Sanders	Independent	Vermont
July–October 1999	Senate	Bob Smith	US Taxpayers	New Hampshire
2000–02	House	Virgil Goode	Independent	Virginia
2001–06	Senate	James Jeffords	Independent	Vermont
2007–12	Senate	Joe Lieberman	Independent Democrat	Connecticut

They don't do much better when it comes to elections for state governors, as Table 2.4 shows. As of January 2011, 49 of the 50 state governors were Democrats or Republicans — all except Lincoln Chafee of Rhode Island, a former Republican senator and the first independent governor of Rhode Island since 1790.

Table 2.4 Third-party state governors since 1990

Years	Name	Party	State
1991–95	Walter Hickel	Alaska Independent	Alaska
1991–95	Lowell Weicker	A Connecticut Party	Connecticut
1995–2003	Angus King	Independent	Maine
1999–2003	Jesse Ventura	Reform	Minnesota
2011–	Lincoln Chafee	Independent	Rhode Island

Obstacles facing third parties   Revised ☐

Third parties in the USA face a number of significant obstacles:

- *The electoral system.* The first-past-the-post, winner-takes-all system, which is used for every election in the USA — federal, state and local — makes life difficult for third parties. For example, Ross Perot won 19% of the vote in 1992 but won no Electoral College votes. This is particularly true of national third parties. Regional third parties, such as George Wallace's American Independent Party in 1968, fare better.

- *Federal campaign finance laws.* The way candidates can qualify for 'matching funds' puts third-party candidates at a disadvantage. Major-party candidates qualify by raising at least $5,000 in contributions of $250 or less in at least 20 states. But third-party candidates qualify only by getting at least 5% of the popular vote. Not only is this a difficult hurdle, but it means that the party can qualify only in the next round of elections. Hence Ross Perot could not qualify for matching funds in 1992, but his Reform Party did qualify in 1996 and 2000 by virtue of getting more than 5% in the previous election.

- *State ballot access laws.* The way third-party candidates have to qualify to get their names on the ballot paper in each state makes life difficult for third parties. States require third-party candidates to present a petition signed by a certain number of registered voters in the state. While Tennessee requires only 25 signatures, in Montana the figure is 5% of all registered voters. This takes time and money.

- *Lack of resources.* Third-party candidates are generally short of resources — especially financial resources. They find fundraising difficult. People are reluctant to give money to parties they see as sure losers, creating something of a 'catch 22' situation.

- *Lack of media coverage.* Third parties also tend to miss out on media coverage. Newspapers and television virtually ignore them. They cannot afford much if anything in the way of television advertisements. They are generally excluded from the televised presidential debates.

- *Lack of well-known, well-qualified candidates.* This again is something of a self-fulfilling prophecy. Third-party candidates are unlikely to be household names and are unlikely to have held any significant political office.

- *Regarded as too ideological.* Because the two major parties are so all-embracing in their ideologies, third parties are often left only the ideological fringes of the political spectrum, as in the case of the Constitution Party or the Socialist Party. Others are easily linked to 'extremism' by their opponents. The following slogan, for example, was used against third-party candidate Governor George Wallace during his 1968 presidential campaign: 'If you liked Hitler, you'll love Wallace.'

- *The tactics of the two major parties.* If a third-party candidate does still manage to win significant support (e.g. Wallace in 1968, Perot in 1992), one or both of the two major parties will eventually adopt some of their policies. So, for example, Nixon pursued what he called his 'southern strategy' in 1972 to woo ex-Wallace voters. Both Governor Bill Clinton and President George H. W. Bush addressed the federal budget deficit issue in the 1992 campaign after Ross Perot had got so much support by talking about it. In this sense, third parties can be seen to be the 'winners' — losing the election but winning the policy debate.

> **Examiner's tip**
>
> Examiners may hint at third parties sometimes being seen to be the 'winners' when they ask questions such as 'Examine the claim that third parties *always lose* in presidential elections.' In an answer to that question you would need to differentiate between third parties always losing the election and often winning the policy argument when their policies are adopted by one or both of the major parties. Make a list of arguments for and against the claim in this question.

Now test yourself

Tested ☐

18 How many current members of Congress are not Democrats or Republicans?

19 How many current state governors are not Democrats or Republicans?

20 List the obstacles faced by third parties.

Answers on p. 108

Exam practice

A Short answer questions:

  1 Which groups of voters tend to support the Republican Party, and why? [15]

  2 Why have conservative Democrats and moderate Republicans both declined as political groups? [15]

  3 Explain the factors that limit the electoral impact of third parties. [15]

B Essay questions:

  1 Examine the claim that political parties in the USA have recently become increasingly ideological. [45]

  2 Why and to what extent does the USA have a two-party system? [45]

  3 Is the distinction between 'red America' and 'blue America' a helpful one? [45]

Answers and quick quiz 2 online

Online ☐

3 Pressure groups

Pressure groups overview

Categories of pressure groups
Revised

Pressure groups are quite distinct from political parties. Whereas political parties seek to win control of government, pressure groups seek to influence those who have won control of government. They vary considerably in terms of size, wealth and influence. Pressure groups in the USA operate at all levels of government — federal, state and local — and seek to bring their influence to bear on all three branches of government: the legislature, the executive and the judiciary. Professor Robert McKeever, a British specialist in US politics, has come up with a helpful categorisation of interest groups and this is shown in Table 3.1.

A **pressure group** is an organised interest group in which members hold similar beliefs and actively pursue ways to influence government.

Typical mistakes

Do be careful, therefore, not to give the Green Party as an example of a pressure group. Greenpeace is a pressure group. The Green Party is, of course, a political party.

Table 3.1 Pressure groups: categories and examples

Type	Example
Business	American Business Conference National Automobile Dealers Association
Agriculture	American Farm Bureau Federation National Farmers Union
Unions	American Federation of Labor and Congress of Industrial Organizations (AFL–CIO) United Auto Workers (UAW)
Professional	American Medical Association American Bar Association
Single issue	Mothers Against Drunk Driving (MADD) National Rifle Association (NRA)
Ideological	American Conservative Union People for the American Way American Civil Liberties Union (ACLU)
Group rights	National Association for the Advancement of Colored People (NAACP) National Organization for Women (NOW) American Association of Retired Persons (AARP)
Public interest	Common Cause Friends of the Earth

Now test yourself

1 Give a definition of a pressure group.
2 What is the difference between a pressure group and a political party?
3 Name four different types of pressure group, and give an example of each.

Tested

Functions of pressure groups
Revised

Pressure groups are said to have five basic functions:

1 *Representation:* they represent the interests of various groups in society. Table 3.1 gives some examples of the types of interest that pressure groups can represent in American politics.

2 *Citizen participation*: they increase the opportunities for ordinary citizens to participate in the decision-making process between elections.

3 *Public education:* they attempt to educate public opinion, warning them of dangers if issues are not addressed. One can see this being done by pressure groups operating in such issue areas as the environment and gun control.

4 *Agenda building:* they attempt to influence the agendas of political parties, legislators and bureaucracies to give prominence and priority to their interests. They will attempt to bring together different parts of American society — for example, business groups, religious groups, state governments, professional organisations — to achieve a common interest.

5 *Programme monitoring:* they will scrutinise and hold government to account in the implementation of policies to try to ensure that promises are fulfilled, policies are actually 'delivered' and regulations are enforced.

Now test yourself

4 What are the five basic functions of pressure groups?
5 What does the function of agenda building involve for a pressure group?

Tested

How pressure groups operate

Revised

Pressure groups use four principal methods to fulfil their functions.

1 *Electioneering and endorsement.* Campaign finance reform has meant that significant changes have taken place in the electioneering and fundraising roles of pressure groups. The 1970s reforms encouraged the setting up of **Political Action Committees** (PACs) — organisations whose purpose is to raise and then give campaign funds to candidates for political office. There is a clear trend that incumbents attract more PAC money than challengers. Pressure groups endorse or oppose candidates for political office based on the candidates' position on the policy areas of concern to them. At election time, groups will often publish voter guides on their websites showing which candidates most closely support the group's stand on issues.

2 *Lobbying.* In order to facilitate **lobbying,** many groups have offices in Washington DC, state capitals and other major US cities. In Washington DC, the lobbyist firms are collectively known as the 'K Street corridor' — named after the street in the city where many lobbyists have their offices. Lobbyists provide policy-makers with information. And for members of Congress, they may also provide them with important voting cues. Many lobbying firms recruit former policy-makers through what is known as 'the revolving door syndrome'.

3 *Publicity.* Lobbying firms launch public relations campaigns to influence the policy-making process. Both the Bush and Obama presidencies have felt the effect of powerful lobbying firms launching publicity blitzes against some of their flagship policies — healthcare and social security reform, to name but two. Publicity campaigns are waged through a number of different means such as television advertisements, journal advertising, roadside hoardings, bumper stickers and badges.

4 *Organising grassroots activities.* These include postal blitzes on members of Congress, the White House or a government department, marches and demonstrations. Most are peaceful, but some may resort to violence.

Examiner's tip

It is easy in writing an essay to give the impression that just because a pressure group exists and does something, it is therefore effective and successful. Do try to be more subtle in your analysis.

Lobbying is an attempt to exert influence on the policy-making, legislative or judicial process by individuals or organised groups.

Now test yourself

6 How do pressure groups get involved in electioneering?
7 What does the term 'lobbying' mean?
8 How do pressure groups run publicity campaigns?
9 What does grassroots organisation involve for a pressure group?

Tested

Political significance of pressure groups

But why are pressure groups so politically significant in American politics? Here are three important reasons:

1 *The USA is a diverse and heterogeneous society.* The United States has been described as a 'melting pot', conveying the picture of all types of diverse groups of people mixed together. The more diverse a society is, the greater will be the variety of special interests to represent. One can see this immediately in the racial mix of American society. Another term used to refer to the USA is that it is the 'hyphenated society'. Everyone seems to have a prefix to their being an 'American', whether it be 'African-American', 'Cuban-American', 'Polish-American', 'Irish-American' or 'Native-American'. And each one has its own pressure group.

2 *The American political system has a great many access points.* In the UK, political power is quite highly centralised. There are few access points for the ordinary citizen to influence government. But in the USA there is a doctrine of 'shared powers' (see p. 55) — shared between the three branches of the federal government as well as between the federal government and the state governments. Even an institution like Congress is fragmented. It is not just in the two chambers that decisions are made, but in the numerous committee rooms as well. There are, therefore, many access points.

3 *The weakness of political parties means that citizens turn more to pressure groups.* In the USA, which has relatively weak, decentralised and undisciplined political parties, parties are not seen as the only groups which organise political activity. It is also quite likely that one party will control the executive and the other party control the legislative branch of the federal government. Democrat Bill Clinton enjoyed party control of Congress for only 2 of his 8 years in office and Republican George W. Bush for only 4½ of his 8 years.

10 How does the diversity of American society affect pressure groups?

11 Give an example of an 'access point' for US pressure groups.

12 What is the link between the comparative weakness of political parties and the significance of pressure groups?

Influence on the federal government

Pressure groups attempt to influence Congress, the executive branch and the courts. American government has far more 'access points' than does government in the UK. Government is thought to be more 'open'. This enhances the potential for influence by pressure groups. And in a system where political parties are clearly weaker than they are in the UK, this again increases opportunities for pressure groups to have greater degrees of influence.

Influence on the legislature

Pressure groups seek to influence the way House and Senate members vote. They do this by a number of methods, including:

● direct contact with House and Senate members and their senior staff

● direct contact with the relevant House and Senate committee members and their staff

- organising constituents to write to, phone, fax, e-mail or visit their House and Senate members to express their support for or opposition to a certain policy initiative
- publicising the voting records of House and Senate members
- endorsement of supportive members and opposition to non-supportive members in forthcoming re-election campaigns
- fundraising, campaigning for or against members of Congress — paying for radio/television advertisements, etc.
- the pressure group EMILY's List supports female congressional candidates, helping them raise money early on in the electoral cycle

Pressure groups may also launch high-profile campaigns in the media when a significant piece of legislation is about to come up for a crucial debate and vote in Congress. Recent examples include congressional debates and votes on healthcare reform, welfare reform, gun control and international environmental agreements (see also p. 80).

Influence on the executive

Revised

Pressure groups seek to maintain strong ties with relevant executive departments, agencies and regulatory commissions. This is especially the case when it comes to the regulatory work of the federal government — regulations, for example, regarding health and safety at work, business, the transport and communications industries or the environment.

Problems can emerge when regulatory bodies are thought to have too cosy a relationship with the particular group they are meant to be regulating. Are they acting as 'watch dogs' or 'lap dogs'?

Edward Ashbee and Nigel Ashford have identified another close link: that between what they call 'producer' groups — such as companies, labour unions or small business federations — and relevant government departments and agencies seeking protection, funding, subsidies or price guarantee mechanisms.

Influence on the judiciary

Revised

Pressure groups can hope to influence the courts by offering *amicus curiae* (friend of the court) briefings. Through these, pressure groups will have an opportunity to present their views to the court in writing before oral arguments are heard. Pressure groups have certainly used this to great effect in recent decades in such areas as the civil rights of racial minorities, abortion rights and First Amendment rights.

The National Association for the Advancement of Colored People (NAACP) was the force behind the landmark Supreme Court decision of *Brown* v. *Board of Education of Topeka* (1954) (see pp. 103–104) as well as the subsequent passage of much civil rights legislation. The NAACP would use its money and professional expertise to bring cases to court for people who could not otherwise afford it. These would be cases that the NAACP believed it could win and which would benefit the interests of

African-Americans. The NAACP has continued to be at the centre of political debate in the USA over affirmative action programmes (see also Topic 4). Pressure groups may actually bring cases themselves, such as the 2005 *McCreary County* v. *American Civil Liberties Union of Kentucky* case.

Both the pro-choice and pro-life lobbies have been active in American politics during the past four decades. Since the 1973 *Roe v. Wade* decision by the Supreme Court (see p. 104), 'pro-choice' groups have fought to preserve the constitutional right of women to have an abortion, whereas 'pro-life' groups have fought to have it both narrowed and overturned. Most recently, they have been involved in the debate concerning the practice of 'partial birth abortions'. In 2000, the Supreme Court refused to allow states to ban these types of abortion. But in 2007, the Supreme Court upheld the ban, declaring it to be constitutional.

The National Rifle Association (NRA) played an important role in the Supreme Court case of *District of Columbia v. Heller* (2008), in which the Court declared unconstitutional the law banning the ownership of handguns in the District.

In the last 20 years, pressure groups have also been active in supporting or opposing the nomination of judges, especially those to the Supreme Court. They were certainly active in the Senate confirmation hearings surrounding Robert Bork (1987) and Clarence Thomas (1991), as well as those of John Roberts (2005) and Samuel Alito (2006).

Typical mistakes

Do beware of mixing 'pro-choice' and 'pro-life'. 'Pro-choice' groups favour giving a woman the right to *choose* whether or not to have an abortion; 'pro-life' groups support the *life* of the unborn child, and are therefore against abortions.

Examiner's tip

Candidates sometimes have the NRA as their only example of a pressure group. Do make sure you have a wide range of examples to use.

Now test yourself

Tested ☐

13 Make a list of the ways in which pressure groups attempt to influence members of Congress
14 What is EMILY's List?
15 What is an *amicus curiae* briefing?
16 Give an example of a Supreme Court case brought by a pressure group.

The debate about pressure groups

Arguments in favour

Revised ☐

There is an important debate about the impact and role of pressure groups in a democracy. *Arguments in favour* of pressure groups having an important role to play in American politics stress that pressure groups provide useful functions, by acting as:

- information-givers — to members of Congress, government departments, the courts and the electorate as a whole, for whom they play an 'educating' role
- policy formulators
- a 'sounding board' for members of Congress and government departments
- enhancers of political participation, especially between elections and on specific issues

Arguments against

Arguments against pressure groups having as much power as they currently seem to have in American politics include the following:

- Money becomes the all-deciding factor — you have to 'pay to play'.
- The late Senator Edward Kennedy once commented that America has 'the finest Congress that money can buy'.
- They work too much for 'special' interests and against the 'national' interest.
- They tend to be elitist and largely unaccountable, and their power thereby detracts from elected (Congress) and accountable (executive) officials.
- They lead to inequalities of power: for example, in policy debates relating to healthcare, tobacco and gun control.
- The 'revolving door syndrome' allows former members of Congress or the executive branch to take up highly paid jobs as lobbyists. This may mean that federal officials use their position to do favours in exchange for an attractive post when they leave office.
- They sometimes use methods of 'direct action' that are deemed by others to be inappropriate: for example, methods used recently by animal rights groups, pro- and anti-abortion groups, environmentalists and anti-capitalist groups.

Debate

For and against pressure groups

Examiner's tip

To help you with questions that ask you for arguments for and against the role that pressure groups play in US politics, construct a two-column table, putting arguments for on one side and arguments against on the other.

Now test yourself

17 What did the late Senator Kennedy say about America and its tie to pressure group money?

18 What is the 'revolving door syndrome'?

Answers on pp. 108–109

Exam practice

A Short answer questions:

    1 In what ways do pressure groups seek to influence Congress, and why? [15]

    2 Why has the impact of professional lobbyists on policy making in the USA been controversial? [15]

    3 What important functions are performed by pressure groups? [15]

B Essay questions:

    1 Examine the claim that 'pressure groups define the political issues that dominate US politics'. [45]

    2 Do pressure groups enhance or hinder democracy in the USA? [45]

    3 Examine the factors that lead to success for a pressure group in Washington DC. [45]

Answers and quick quiz 3 online

4 Racial and ethnic politics

Racial and ethnic diversity in the USA

Changes in the US population
Revised

In the beginning, the USA was a creation of white European Protestants. Black people were, in most cases, slaves; Native Americans were not regarded as citizens either. During the nineteenth and twentieth centuries all that changed.

- The end of the Civil War (1865) brought the emancipation of the slaves.
- Immigration through the nineteenth and twentieth centuries brought a flood of new settlers: Irish Catholics; European Jews; Hispanics from Mexico and other Central American countries; refugees from Africa, the Middle East and Asia.
- During the 1990s, the combined population of African-Americans, Native Americans, Asians, Pacific Islanders and Hispanic/Latinos grew at 13 times the rate of the non-Hispanic white population.
- The 2010 census showed Hispanics (16.3%) as a larger proportion of the US population than African-Americans (12.3%).
- But racial and ethnic diversity varies hugely from state to state: Vermont is 95% white, while Hawaii is just 24% white; Mississippi is 37% black, while Montana is just 0.4% black; New Mexico is 46% Hispanic, while West Virginia is just 1.2% Hispanic.
- The Hispanic population grew by 43% between 2000 and 2010; the African-American population grew by just 12% during the same period.
- Four states — New Mexico, Texas, California and Hawaii — are majority-minority states in which minorities make up a majority of the state's population.
- It is estimated that by 2025 the Hispanic and Asian communities will make up more than one-quarter of the US population.
- All this has had and will have great significance for government and politics in the USA.

Now test yourself

1. What are the two main causes of increased racial and ethnic diversity in the USA?
2. Name four ethnic groups who arrived in the USA during the nineteenth and twentieth centuries.
3. What was surprising about the numbers of African-Americans and Hispanics in the 2010 census?
4. Name two of the four states in which racial and ethnic minorities now form a majority of the population.

Tested

The civil rights movement and minority political activism

Civil rights
Revised

The **civil rights** movement grew out of the 1950s. The post-Civil War period had seen the passage of the 13th, 14th and 15th

Amendments guaranteeing rights for African-Americans, but laws in many states — especially in the Deep South — meant that these rights were not a reality for most blacks. Whether in schools, housing, job recruitment, public transport or leisure facilities, blacks were still 'separate but equal' at best; a discriminated against and persecuted minority at worst.

The civil rights movement was initially characterised by peaceful protest against government-sponsored segregation and was played out on the streets and in the court rooms, rather than in the debating chambers of Congress or the federal offices of Washington DC.

The highlights of the movement included:
- the Supreme Court's ruling in *Brown v. Board of Education of Topeka* (1954) (see pp. 103–104)
- the bus boycotts and freedom riders in the South following the arrest of Rosa Parks (1955)
- the March for Jobs and Freedom in Washington DC, including Martin Luther King's 'I have a dream' speech (1963)
- the assassination of Martin Luther King (1968)
- the Million Man March in Washington DC (1995)

The civil rights movement was divided into a number of differing factions, some peaceful, some violent, each with its own leaders, including:
- Martin Luther King and the Southern Christian Leadership Conference
- Malcolm X and (later) Louis Farrakhan and the Nation of Islam movement
- Jesse Jackson and the National Rainbow Coalition
- the National Association for the Advancement of Colored People (NAACP)

> **Civil rights** are positive acts of government designed to protect persons against arbitrary or discriminatory treatment by government or individuals.

Examiner's tip

In essays, don't spend too much time on the historical background. Concentrate on the more contemporary material.

Typical mistakes

Some candidates have only *Brown v. Board of Education of Topeka* to offer. Although it is a landmark decision, it was made nearly 60 years ago. Ensure you also use more up-to-date examples.

Now test yourself

5 Define the term 'civil rights'.
6 Name three of the historic landmark events of the civil rights movement between 1955 and 1995.
7 Name three of the important leaders of the civil rights movement during this period.

Tested

Affirmative action

Brief history   Revised

The debate centres on whether society should be aiming for **equality of opportunity** or **equality of results**. From the mid-twentieth century, many civil rights advocates came to believe that equality of opportunity would not in itself guarantee equality for minority groups. They would have rights only in theory, not in practice. Only equality of results would truly deliver equality for racial and ethnic minorities. Hence the movement towards what would become known as **affirmative action** programmes.

In March 1961, President Kennedy created the Equal Employment Opportunity Commission. Kennedy ordered that projects financed with federal funds 'take affirmative action' to ensure that hiring and employment practices would be free from racial bias. President Johnson used the same phrase in 1965 regarding federal government contractors.

But affirmative action soon attracted its critics. Many regarded 'set asides' and 'quotas' as unfair to those of the majority group — whites — and patronising to those of the minority. Some used the term **reverse**

> **Affirmative action** is a programme that entails giving the members of a previously disadvantaged minority group a head start in such areas as higher education and employment.

discrimination — a term closely associated with the 1978 Supreme Court case of *Regents of the University of California* v. *Bakke*, which concerned a white medical student, Allan Bakke, who had been denied a place at the University of California's Medical School, despite the fact that lesser-qualified minority students were admitted. Other landmark Supreme Court cases on affirmative action included:

- *Adarand Constructors* v. *Peña* (1995)
- *Gratz* v. *Bollinger* (2003)
- *Parents Involved in Community Schools Inc.* v. *Seattle School District No. 1* (2007)
- *Meredith* v. *Jefferson County (Kentucky) Board of Education* (2007)

(These cases are discussed on p. 104.)

James Q. Wilson and John DiLulio (*American Government*, 2001) summarise the position on affirmative action as follows:

- The courts will subject any quota system created by state or local governments to 'strict scrutiny' and will be looking for a 'compelling' justification for it.
- **Quotas** or preference systems cannot be used by state or local governments without first showing that such rules are needed to correct an actual past or present pattern of discrimination.
- In proving that there has been discrimination, it is not enough to show that racial or ethnic minorities are statistically under-represented among employees, etc.
- Quotas or preference systems that are created by federal, rather than state, law will be given greater deference.

> **Quotas** are a set-aside programme to benefit previously disadvantaged minorities in such areas as higher education and employment by which a certain percentage (i.e. quota) of places is reserved for people of the previously disadvantaged group.

Arguments for and against affirmative action

Revised

There are six arguments put forward in favour of affirmative action. They are that affirmative action:

1 leads to greater levels of diversity and **multiculturalism**
2 rights previous wrongs — the previously disadvantaged are now advantaged
3 opens up areas of education and employment that minorities would not otherwise have considered
4 creates a diverse student body in educational establishments that promotes racial tolerance
5 is the most effective way of delivering equality of opportunity
6 works — for example, between 1960 and 1995, the percentage of black people aged 25–29 who graduated from university rose from 5% to 15%

There are six arguments put forward against affirmative action. They are that:

1 Advantage or preference for one group leads inevitably to disadvantage for another group — the issue of 'reverse discrimination'.
2 Affirmative action can lead to minorities being admitted to courses/jobs for which they are ill-equipped to cope.
3 Such programmes can be condescending to minorities, implying that they need extra help to succeed, thereby demeaning their achievements.

> **Debate**
>
> For and against affirmative action

> **Multiculturalism:** the existence within a nation state of people from many different cultures whose own learned patterns of behaviour lead to a diversity of culture in such matters as lifestyle, belief, custom and language.

> **Examiner's tip**
>
> When you are presenting arguments for and against, be careful not to state things so categorically in the 'for' argument that in the 'against' argument you contradict yourself. Use phrases such as: 'on the one hand...on the other hand...'; 'some argue that... while others argue that...'.

4 Affirmative action perpetuates a society based on colour and race, thereby encouraging prejudice.

5 It is no more than a quota system under another name.

6 It focuses on groups rather than individuals.

Has affirmative action been a success?

Revised

In 1995, President Clinton declared that 'affirmative action has been good for America'. Was he right in this? Before answering that, we must first establish what it was meant to achieve. Affirmative action was meant to move society towards a time when previously disadvantaged groups would no longer be disadvantaged and therefore such programmes would no longer be required. Affirmative action programmes are therefore best seen as a means to an end, not as an end in themselves. So how successful have such programmes been by this measure? There is evidence on both sides.

Some argue that affirmative action programmes have failed because a programme that is based on race is unlikely to move society to a point where race no longer counts. But others argue that by promoting diversity, racial tolerance has been enhanced and old prejudices are slowly dying. The election of Barack Obama as president of the USA would doubtless be presented as evidence that society is moving on from its once ingrained prejudices.

One must also bear in mind whether the costs of affirmative action programmes outweigh their benefits. If, after all, under-prepared blacks or Hispanics are put into academic institutions or jobs where they do not succeed, then the cost may be too high and the programme seen as a failure. If many Americans refuse to visit a black doctor or dentist because they assume that he or she was admitted to medical school and to the position they now hold through quotas rather than qualifications, then the cost may again be too high. Some research has found evidence of such problems. Furthermore, affirmative action can be something of a blunt instrument — one that is too undiscriminating. After all, why should Obama's daughters be admitted to college ahead of the son or daughter of a (white) West Virginian coal miner?

In the 2003 *Bollinger* decisions, the Supreme Court suggested that affirmative action programmes ought to have a shelf life of a further 25 years. By that reckoning, we shall be better able to judge the success or failure of affirmative action programmes in 2028!

Examiner's tip

To help you with questions that ask you for arguments for and against affirmative action, construct a two-column table, putting arguments for on one side and arguments against on the other.

Now test yourself

8 What is affirmative action?

9 What is reverse discrimination?

10 What are quotas?

11 Define the term 'multiculturalism'.

Tested

Minority representation in the federal government

In 1992, President-elect Bill Clinton talked about having a cabinet that 'looks like America'. To what extent do the various branches of the federal government 'look like America' in terms of minority representation?

Minorities in Congress

In 1984, there were 21 African-Americans in Congress — all in the House of Representatives. In 2011, there were 42 African-American members of Congress — all in the House — and African-American James Clyburn of South Carolina, formerly House Majority Whip, became Assistant House Democratic Leader. In 2007–08, when the Democrats controlled the House, five House committee chairmanships were filled by African-Americans. The rise in African-American members of the House was brought about largely by the creation in some states of majority-minority districts in the early 1990s. In 2011, there were also 28 Hispanics in Congress — 26 in the House and two in the Senate — compared with just 10 (all in the House) in 1984.

Minorities and presidential elections

The last 40 years have witnessed the following milestones for African-Americans running for the presidency:

- 1972: Representative Shirley Chisholm (D) became the first major-party African-American candidate for the presidency. She won 152 delegates at her party's National Convention.
- 1984: Civil rights activist Jesse Jackson (D) won over 3 million votes in the Democratic primaries, finishing third in the number of votes cast. Jackson became the first African-American candidate to win a major-party presidential primary, winning contests in four states plus the District of Columbia.
- 1988: Jackson ran again for the Democratic nomination, winning contests in ten states plus Washington DC.
- 2008: Senator Barack Obama (D) became the first black major-party presidential candidate and went on to defeat Republican John McCain to win the presidency.

Between 1992 and 2008, African-American voters gave at least 83% of their votes to the Democratic presidential candidate, rising to 95% in 2008. During the same period, Hispanic voters gave at least 62% of their votes to the Democratic presidential candidate in four of the five elections held in those 16 years. The only election in which the Hispanic vote for the Democrats fell below that figure was 2004, when John Kerry attracted only 57% of the Hispanic vote, with Republican President George W. Bush capturing 43% of the Hispanic vote. But that figure fell back to just 31% for Republican John McCain in 2008 with the Democrat vote up to 67%.

Minorities in the executive branch

Minority representation in the president's cabinet first became an issue in modern times when President Lyndon Johnson appointed African-American Robert Weaver as Secretary of Housing and Urban Development in 1966. Between 1966 and 2009, 16 other African-Americans were appointed to head executive departments, including two of the last three secretaries of state — Colin Powell (2001–05) and Condoleezza Rice (2005–09) — and Barack Obama's first Attorney General, Eric Holder.

Obama's incoming cabinet in January 2009 was the most racially diverse of any administration, with heads of seven of the 15 executive departments being from racial minorities:

- African-American: Eric Holder (Justice)
- Hispanics: Ken Salazar (Interior) and Hilda Solis (Labor)
- Chinese-Americans: Steven Chu (Energy) and Gary Locke (Commerce — now US Ambassador to China)
- Japanese-American: Eric Shinseki (Veterans Affairs)
- Lebanese-American: Ray LaHood (Transportation)

Minorities in the judiciary

Revised

Not only did President Lyndon Johnson appoint the first African-American to the cabinet, but in 1967 he also appointed the first African-American to the Supreme Court — Thurgood Marshall. Upon Marshall's retirement in 1991, President George H. W. Bush replaced him with another African-American, Clarence Thomas. In 1986, President Reagan had appointed the first Italian-American to the Supreme Court — Antonin Scalia.

During President Reagan's 8 years in office (1981–89), less than 5% of his appointees to the federal judiciary were from racial minorities. But during President Clinton's 8 years (1993–2001), over 23% of federal judiciary appointees were from racial minorities. Nine per cent of President George W. Bush's federal judicial appointees were Hispanics, and during his first 2 years, Obama's judicial appointees were 27.5% African-American and 7.1% Hispanic.

Now test yourself

Tested

12 To what extent has African-American and Hispanic representation increased in Congress since the 1980s?
13 How has the voting pattern of Hispanics changed in recent elections?
14 Give four examples of people of minority race in Obama's 2009 cabinet.
15 How have appointments to the federal judiciary changed from President Reagan to President Obama?

Answers on p. 109

Exam practice

A Short answer questions:
  1 Why do some people in the USA oppose affirmative action? [15]
  2 What is affirmative action and what are the justifications for it? [15]
  3 To what extent has racial and ethnic minority representation increased in the federal government during the past 30 years? [15]
B Essay questions:
  1 How important was the election of a black president in 2008 in overcoming racial divisions in the USA? [45]
  2 Examine the claim that 'affirmative action is bound to fail because it is based on race'. [45]
  3 Discuss the impact of affirmative action in the USA and explain why it has attracted growing criticism. [45]

Answers and quick quiz 4 online

Online

5 The Constitution

Nature of the Constitution

Background to the Constitution

Revised

In order to understand the nature of the Constitution, we need to know something about what came before it. Here is a brief survey of what occurred in the years before the writing of the Constitution:

- 1776: the 13 colonies on the eastern seaboard of North America declared their independence from Great Britain in the Declaration of Independence.
- 1776–83: there followed the War of Independence between the former colonies and Great Britain.
- 1781: the newly independent colonies decided to establish a **confederacy** — a loose association of states in which almost all political power rests with the individual states — by the Articles of Confederation.
- 1787: because the confederacy had proved a disaster with insufficient power for the national government, the Philadelphia Convention convened to draw up a new constitution.
- This involved making a whole number of compromises in terms of the allocation of national government power and state government power.

Compromises of the Constitution

Revised

The form of government

- Under British control, the colonies had been ruled under a **unitary** form of government. A unitary form of government is one in which political power rests with one central/national government (of Great Britain in this case).
- From 1781 they had been ruled by a **confederal** form of government. A confederal form of government is one in which virtually all political power rests with the individual states, and little with the central/national government.
- The compromise was to devise a new form of government — a **federal** form of government. A federal form of government is one in which some political power rests with the national (or federal) government but other, equally important, powers rest with the state governments.

Representation of the states

- Large-population states wanted representation in Congress to be **proportional to population**: the bigger the population of a state, the more representatives it would have in the new Congress.

> **Examiner's tip**
>
> Notice 'equally important' — not just trivial matters such as keeping the roads clean.

> **Typical mistakes**
>
> Don't use the phrase 'proportional representation'; it isn't. Proportional representation refers to a voting system; allocating seats in the House to the states in proportion to their population is something quite different.

- Small-population states wanted **equal representation**.
- The compromise was to have a Congress made up of two houses — the House of Representatives and the Senate.
- In the House of Representatives, there would be representation proportional to population.
- In the Senate, there would be equal representation for all states, regardless of population.

Choosing of the president

- There were many different suggestions about how to choose the president.
- Some thought the president should be appointed.
- Others thought the president should be directly elected by the people.
- The compromise was to have the president **indirectly elected** by an Electoral College (see pp. 18–19).
- The people would elect the Electoral College and the 'Electors' within the Electoral College would choose the president.

> **Examiner's tip**
> Use 'Electors' with a capital 'E' to avoid confusing them with 'electors' (i.e. ordinary voters).

A codified constitution

Revised

The new Constitution was to be a **codified constitution**. This would be in sharp contrast to Great Britain's largely unwritten and entirely uncodified constitution. The new Constitution would enumerate certain powers that the national (federal) government would possess and leave all other powers to the states or the people. It would also contain a deliberately complicated and demanding amendment process. Amendments to the Constitution were permitted, but only if they were overwhelmingly desired by both the federal and the state governments.

> **A codified constitution** is a constitution that consists of a full and authoritative set of rules written down in a single text.

But although the US Constitution is rightly described as codified, there are phrases within it which were written deliberately vaguely and which have 'evolved' over the subsequent decades and centuries. So, for example, the Constitution allows Congress:

- 'to provide for the common defence and **general welfare** of the United States'
- 'to make all laws which shall be **necessary and proper** for carrying into execution the foregoing powers'

These two clauses — known as the 'general welfare clause' and the 'necessary and proper clause' — have allowed the powers of the federal government to expand significantly over time. The Constitution has also changed significantly since the late eighteenth century by virtue of:

- formal amendment: e.g. permitting a federal income tax (16th Amendment, 1913) — see p. 61
- interpretative amendment: by the Supreme Court's power of judicial review — see pp. 100–101

However, just because the United States has a codified constitution does not mean that everything to do with US government and politics is in the Constitution. You will, for example, find nothing in the Constitution about:

- presidential primaries
- congressional committees
- the president's cabinet
- the Executive Office of the President
- the Supreme Court's power of judicial review

Now test yourself

1 What is the difference between unitary, confederal and federal forms of government?
2 Give three examples of compromises in the Constitution.
3 What is a codified constitution?
4 Give two examples of the vagueness of the Constitution.
5 Give two examples of things to do with US government and politics which are not mentioned in the Constitution.

Principles of the Constitution

The Constitution can be said to be based on three principles: separation of powers; checks and balances; the federal division of powers. The first two must be understood together as the one is a corollary of the other.

Separation of powers

Revised

The Constitution drawn up at Philadelphia in 1787 divided the national government into three branches based on what is known as the doctrine of the **separation of powers**. The three branches of government are:

- the **legislature**: Congress, which makes the laws
- the **executive**: headed by the president, which carries out the laws
- the **judiciary**: headed by the Supreme Court, which enforces and interprets the laws

The idea of the Founding Fathers was that these three branches would:

- be independent yet co-equal
- be separate in terms of personnel
- operate checks and balances on each other
- promote the much desired concept of **limited government** — as Thomas Jefferson (one of the Founding Fathers) put it: 'that government is best which governs least'

The framers of the Constitution believed that only by these kinds of institutional structure would tyranny be avoided. It was in their view of vital importance that law making, law executing and law enforcing be carried out by three independent yet co-equal bodies whose personnel was entirely separate. Thus was introduced what might be called the separation of personnel — that the legislature, the executive and the judiciary should

> **Separation of powers** is a theory of government whereby political power is distributed among three branches of government — the legislature, the executive and the judiciary — acting both independently and interdependently.
>
> **Limited government** is the principle that the size and scope of the federal government should be limited to that which is necessary only for the common good of the people.

Typical mistakes

Do watch the spelling of 'separation'. An easy way to remember the correct spelling is that it has two 'a's in the middle.

all be separately manned; that no person be permitted to be a member of more than one branch at any one time. Hence in January 2009:

- Barack Obama resigned from the Senate to become president
- Joe Biden resigned from the Senate to become vice-president
- Hillary Clinton resigned from the Senate to join Obama's cabinet as Secretary of State

All three resigned from the legislature in order to join the executive. And when in 2010 the US Solicitor General Elena Kagan was appointed to the Supreme Court, Ms Kagan resigned from the executive in order to join the judiciary.

Checks and balances

Revised

But the functions of these three branches are not completely separate. Indeed, the term 'separation of powers' is rather confusing for it is not the powers that are separate but the *institutions*. As Richard Neustadt has stated: 'The Constitutional Convention of 1787 is supposed to have created a government of "separated powers". It did nothing of the sort. Rather, it created a government of separated institutions sharing powers.'

So the theory is more accurately described as a theory of **shared powers** than 'separated powers'. The institutions — the Congress, the presidency and the courts — are indeed separate. The personnel of these three branches are separate but their powers are shared. This sharing of powers is what we call **checks and balances**. The way in which each branch checks and balances the others is shown in Table 5.1.

Examiner's tip

The phrase 'shared powers' is a much more accurate description of American government than 'separated powers'.

Checks and balances is a system of government in which each branch — legislative, executive and judicial — exercises control over the actions of the other branches of government.

Table 5.1 Checks and balances

Checks by	Checks on		
	The legislature	The executive	The judiciary
The legislature		• Amend/delay/reject the president's legislation • Override the president's veto • Control of the budget • Senate's power to confirm numerous appointments made by the president • Senate's power to ratify treaties negotiated by the president • Declare war • Investigation • Impeachment, trial, conviction and removal from office of any member of the executive branch, including the president	• Senate's power to confirm appointments made by the president • Initiate constitutional amendments • Impeachment, trial, conviction and removal from office of any member of the judiciary
The executive	• Recommend legislation • Veto legislation • Call Congress into special session		• Appointment of judges • Pardon
The judiciary	• Judicial review: the power to declare Acts of Congress unconstitutional	• Judicial review: the power to declare actions of any member of the executive branch — including the president — unconstitutional	

Federal division of powers

The third principle upon which the Constitution is based is the federal division of powers. Federalism involves a certain level of **decentralisation**. As already explained, it is a compromise between a centralised form of government on the one hand and a loose confederation of independent states on the other. In other words, it is a compromise between the two experiences America had before 1787 — government by Great Britain and government by the Articles of Confederation. It is an appropriate form of government for a country as large and diverse as the USA. It allows for national unity as well as regional and local diversity.

Nowhere are the words 'federal' or 'federalism' to be found in the American Constitution. It is written into the Constitution by:

● Articles I, II and III, which lay out the powers of the national government
● Amendment X, which guarantees that all the remaining powers 'are reserved to the states and to the people'.

What the Constitution does is to:

● Give certain **exclusive powers** to the national (federal) government. Only the national government can, for example, coin money, negotiate treaties, tax imports and exports, or maintain troops in peacetime.

● Give guarantees of **states' rights**. So, for example, the states are guaranteed equal representation in the Senate, that their borders will not be changed without their consent and that the Constitution cannot be amended without the agreement of three-quarters of them.

● Make clear that there are also **states' responsibilities**. Each state must recognise the laws of each other state by, for example, returning fugitives.

All this the Constitution did. But what it failed to do — and wisely so — was to lay down any definite line between the concurrent powers of the national and state governments. This means that the concept of federalism has been able to develop over the subsequent two centuries.

> **Decentralisation** is the principle by which government and political power are vested not only in the federal government, but also in the state governments.
>
> **States' rights,** literally, are the rights, powers and duties of the state governments, but the term is often used to denote opposition to increasing the federal government's power at the expense of that of the states.

> **Examiner's tip**
>
> It is the 10th Amendment that is so much stressed by supporters of the Tea Party movement because they want to see the federal government doing less.

Now test yourself

6 Define the doctrine of the separation of powers.
7 What is meant by limited government?
8 What is meant by checks and balances?
9 Complete this quotation: 'separated institutions, sharing _____' (one word).
10 What is meant by decentralisation?
11 What is meant by states' rights?

Federalism

Development of federalism

Federalism, therefore, is not a fixed concept; it is ever changing. As America has changed, so has the concept of federalism.

Exam practice answers and quick quizzes at **www.therevisionbutton.co.uk/myrevisionnotes**

The most significant changes that have occurred in the USA since 1787 and have led to the development and evolution of federalism are:

- westward expansion
- the growth in population
- industrialisation
- improvements in communication — by road, rail, air, post, telephone, radio, television, e-mail etc.
- America's foreign policy role and world-power status

During the latter part of the nineteenth century and the first two-thirds of the twentieth century, all these five factors led to an increased role for the federal government and a decline in the power of state governments. But during the final third of the twentieth century, there was a distinct move in the opposite direction as Americans wanted to see more power and more decisions devolved to the states wherever this was possible. It is therefore possible to discern three distinct phases of federalism in America:

1 **Dual federalism** (1780s–1920s) — an era in which the state governments had significant power.

2 **Cooperative federalism** (1930s–1960s) — an era in which the federal government became more and more powerful, sometimes at the expense of the states. This is associated with the Democratic presidents Franklin Roosevelt, Truman, Kennedy and Johnson, as well as with the USA becoming a world power. The federal government administered **categorical grants**, schemes by which Washington was able to stipulate how federal tax dollars were used by the states.

3 **New federalism** (1970s–present) — an era in which, wherever possible, power was devolved to the states. This is associated with the Republican Presidents Nixon, Ford, Reagan and George H. W. Bush, but was also partly adopted by Clinton in the 1990s. The federal government gradually moved towards **block grants** and **revenue sharing**, by which Washington allowed the states greater independence in how federal tax dollars were spent.

As a result of policies pursued by administrations of both parties — though especially Republicans — over the last 40 years, the states have seen quite a significant increase in their autonomy and power. Decentralisation and states' rights are once again the buzzwords in American politics. This has come about through:

- the reduction of federal government economic aid to the states
- a perception that federal government programmes such as FDR's New Deal and Johnson's Great Society had not been as successful as first thought
- a belief that the federal government had simply failed to tackle some pressing social problems, such as those associated with gun crime, drugs, abortion, welfare and poverty, leading to a widespread distrust and scepticism of the federal government and 'Washington politicians'
- decisions by the mainly Republican-appointed Supreme Court, which began to limit the scope of the federal government in such cases as *United States* v. *Lopez* (1995) and *Printz* v. *United States* (1997), while upholding states' rights in such cases as *Webster* v. *Reproductive Health*

> **Federalism** is a theory of government by which political power is divided between a national government and state governments, each having their own areas of substantive jurisdiction.

Typical mistakes

Don't get carried away in your essays with the history of federalism. Concentrate on what happened under the most recent presidents – mainly Bush and Obama. See pp. 58 and 59.

Services (1989) and *Planned Parenthood of Southeastern Pennsylvania* v. *Casey* (1992) (see pp. 102–104 for details)

- the Republican domination of the White House during the 1970s and 1980s, and again during the first 8 years of this century, and control of Congress between 1995 and 2006, which allowed conservative politicians to push their states' rights agenda
- the election of a significant number of Republican state governors since the mid-1990s, which led to state-based innovations in such policy areas as the environment and healthcare

Federalism under George W. Bush

Revised

You would expect a Republican president to be keen on decentralisation and giving more power to the state governments. You would certainly expect that of a Republican president who had been governor of Texas for 6 years before entering the White House. But that wasn't what happened. During the presidency of George W. Bush (2001–09), federal government spending grew at a rate not seen since the days of President Johnson in the 1960s — and he was a Democrat. Whereas former Republican presidents had arrived in Washington determined to cut federal government bureaucracy, George W. Bush expanded it.

There are five particular reasons for this expansion of the federal government under George W. Bush:

1 the war in Iraq
2 homeland security issues following the attacks on the USA on 9/11 (2001)
3 the expansion of the Medicare programme
4 the No Child Left Behind Act passed by Congress (2001)
5 the Wall Street and banking collapse (2008)

Not all Republicans agreed with Bush's huge expansion of federal government spending. Even some of his own party derided such programmes as '**big-government conservatism**'. Bush was widely criticised by many conservative Republicans for not vetoing expensive federal government programmes. He failed to use a single veto during his entire first term (2001–05), the first president to do so since Martin Van Buren (1837–41). Bush was also criticised for what many saw as the federal government's somewhat feeble initial response to the devastation caused by Hurricane Katrina in 2005.

Finally, when in 2008 the Bush White House authorised the secretary of the treasury, Henry Paulson, to take control of two troubled, privately owned but government-sponsored mortgage companies — known colloquially as Fannie Mae and Freddie Mac — there was more criticism heaped on Bush, by conservative Republicans in particular. This was followed by a Bush White House-sponsored $700 billion 'bail-out' package for Wall Street to alleviate the effects of the credit crunch. The legislation passed through Congress but with mainly Democrat votes.

In 1996 Bill Clinton had commented that the era of big government was over. By the end of the George W. Bush administration, it was clear that it was back.

Federalism under Barack Obama

Whereas the Bush administration concentrated mainly on war and terrorism, the Obama White House is clearly much more focused on domestic policy as a way of delivering his 'change' agenda. This has a profound effect on the relationship between Washington and the states. War and security against terrorism are conducted exclusively by the federal government; domestic policy is increasingly the domain of the states. Thus the following trends in federalism have so far been seen during the Obama presidency:

- The ratio of state and local government employees to federal employees is the highest since before Roosevelt's New Deal in the 1930s.
- Federal government assistance to the states increased from 3.7% of gross domestic product (GDP) in 2008 to 4.6% of GDP in 2009.
- Money from the federal government accounted for 30% of state government spending in 2009 compared with 25% in 2008.
- Of the $787 billion of the 2009 Economic Stimulus Package, one-third ($246 billion) went to or through the state governments. (Under Bush's 2003 stimulus package, just $20 billion went to the states.)

There are a number of reasons for the increase in federal money to the states under the Obama administration:

- the re-authorisation of the State Children's Health Insurance Program (SCHIP) (2009)
- the expansion of Medicaid under Obama's healthcare reform legislation
- higher education expenditure (e.g. Pell Grants, 2010)
- $4.35 billion invested in the Race to the Top program to boost education in the states

Obama came in for a good deal of criticism for his view of federalism. Many Republicans saw the passage of the healthcare reform legislation as 'the end of federalism' and there were those in the Tea Party movement who thought Obama more of a socialist than a federalist. In exit polls at the 2010 mid-term elections, 74% of Republicans and 60% of independents agreed with the statement that 'the federal government is doing too many things better left to businesses and individuals'.

Consequences of federalism

You should be aware of the way in which federalism affects many aspects of US government and politics. Here are a few important ways:

- variation in state laws concerning such matters as the age at which one can drive a car and must attend school
- variation in penalties for law breaking from state to state
- complexity of the American legal system, having both national and state courts
- each state having not only its own laws and courts but also its own Constitution

- complexity of the tax system: income tax (federal and state); state property taxes; local sales taxes
- state-based elections, run largely under state law (see p. 9)
- the frequency and number of elections
- political parties being decentralised and largely state based (see pp. 29–30)
- regional diversity (the South, Midwest, Northeast, etc.) and regional considerations when making appointments to, for example, the cabinet, or when 'balancing the ticket' in the presidential election (see p. 22)

Now test yourself

Tested

12 Give a definition of federalism.

13 Over the last 40 years, has the government of the USA become more centralised or more decentralised?

14 Name three reasons/events which led to George W. Bush expanding the role of the federal government.

15 Name three things for which Bush was criticised, especially by conservatives.

16 What had President Clinton said about 'the era of big government' back in 1996?

17 Give two reasons for the increase in federal money to the states under Obama.

18 What piece of legislation led Republicans to claim that Obama had presided over 'the end of federalism'?

The constitutional framework

The Constitution in outline

Revised

The Constitution today is made up of the original seven articles plus 27 amendments, 10 of which were added almost immediately. Of the original seven articles, the first three are the most important:

- Article I: the legislature, including the powers of Congress (Section 8)
- Article II: the executive, including the powers of the president (Section 2)
- Article III: the judiciary

The first ten amendments, added in 1791, are known collectively as the **Bill of Rights**, as they enumerate fundamental rights and freedoms. The most significant are:

- 1st: freedom of religion, speech and the press, and the right to peaceful assembly
- 2nd: right to keep and bear arms
- 4th: freedom from unreasonable searches
- 5th: rights of accused persons (including the 'due process' clause)
- 8th: freedom from cruel and unusual punishments
- 10th: rights reserved to the states and to the people

Since 1791, just 17 further amendments have been added. Two of these — the 18th and the 21st — cancel each other out. The 18th introduced the prohibition of alcohol (1919) and the 21st repealed that amendment (1933). Of the remaining 15 amendments, the following are the most significant:

- 14th: guarantees of 'equal protection' and 'due process' applied to all states
- 16th: Congress given power to tax income
- 17th: direct election of senators
- 22nd: two-term limit for president
- 25th: presidential disability and succession

The amendment process — Revised

Amending the Constitution is a two-stage process: proposal and ratification (see Table 5.2).

1 Proposals to amend the Constitution can be made either by Congress with a two-thirds majority in favour in both houses, or by a national Constitutional Convention called at the request of two-thirds of the state legislatures. The latter has never been used.

2 Ratification can be made either by three-quarters of the state legislatures or by three-quarters of the states holding a Constitutional Convention. The latter has been used only once — to ratify the 21st Amendment in 1933.

Typical mistakes
You must say 'a two-thirds majority *in both houses*'.

Typical mistakes
Note that this three-quarters figure concerns the proportion of states that must ratify, not the majority by which they must ratify the amendment.

Table 5.2 Procedures for amending the Constitution

Amendments proposed by:	Amendments ratified by:
Either	Either
Congress: two-thirds majority in both houses required	**State legislatures:** three-quarters of the state legislatures must vote to ratify, often within a stated time limit
or	or
National Constitutional Convention: called by at least two-thirds of the states (never used)	**State Constitutional Conventions:** three-quarters of the states must hold Conventions and vote to ratify

Typical mistakes
Don't say that 'Congress can amend the Constitution'. It cannot. Congress can 'propose constitutional amendments'.

Six amendments have been proposed by Congress but failed at the ratification stage, the most recent being one to guarantee equal rights for women, proposed by Congress in 1972 but ratified by only 35 states — three short of the required three-quarters. Many amendments have failed at the proposal stage. Recent examples include proposals to:

- require the federal government to pass a balanced budget
- impose term limits on members of Congress
- forbid desecration of the American flag

So, why has the Constitution been so rarely amended? There are five main reasons:

1 The Founding Fathers created a deliberately difficult amendment process.

2 The vagueness of the Constitution has allowed the document to evolve without the need for constant formal amendment.

3 The Supreme Court's power of judicial review allows the Court to amend the meaning of the Constitution while the words remain largely unaltered (see Topic 8).

Examiner's tip
Do notice that a question about amending the US Constitution could require quite a substantial piece on the Supreme Court's power of judicial review. Remember always, therefore, to think across the eight topics: don't regard them as water-tight compartments. They often interrelate, so your answers will often need to reflect that.

4 The reverence with which the Constitution is regarded makes many politicians cautious of tampering with it.

5 The 18th Amendment, regarding the prohibition of alcohol, was repealed (by the 21st Amendment) just 14 years later.

Now test yourself Tested

19 What do the first three articles of the Constitution talk about?
20 What are the first 10 amendments to the Constitution called?
21 Give brief details of two subsequent amendments to the Constitution (i.e. post-1791).
22 How can constitutional amendments be proposed?
23 How can constitutional amendments be ratified?
24 Give two examples of proposals that have failed.
25 Give the five reasons why there have been so few constitutional amendments.

Constitutional rights

Revised

As we have seen, the Constitution guarantees certain fundamental rights. These **constitutional rights** can be thought of in two categories: freedom of or to, and freedom from (see Table 5.3). But a list of rights tells us nothing about their effectiveness. In order for these rights to be effective, the government — be it federal, state or local — must take steps to ensure that the rights are effectively protected. When it comes to the federal government, all three branches of government need to be involved.

Constitutional rights are the fundamental rights guaranteed by the federal Constitution, principally in the Bill of Rights — the first 10 amendments — but also in subsequent amendments.

- Congress can pass laws to facilitate these rights — laws that enhance the rights of, for example, racial minorities. It can also, through its committee system and investigative powers, call the executive branch to account regarding the way it implements the laws that Congress has passed (see p. 67).
- The executive branch needs to implement the laws and programmes which Congress passes and establishes in order to ensure that legislation is followed by delivery.
- The Supreme Court has an important role in safeguarding the constitutional rights of citizens through its power of judicial review (see pp. 100–101).

Table 5.3 Classification of constitutional rights

Freedom of/to:	Freedom from:
Speech (1st Amendment)	Unreasonable searches (4th Amendment)
Religion (1st Amendment)	
The press (1st Amendment)	Cruel and unusual punishment (8th Amendment)
Assembly (1st Amendment)	
Keep and bear arms (2nd Amendment)	Excessive bail (8th Amendment)
Remain silent (5th Amendment)	Slavery and involuntary servitude (13th Amendment)
Speedy and public trial (6th Amendment)	
Vote (over-18s) (26th Amendment)	

Of these three branches of government, it is the judiciary — and in the end the Supreme Court — which plays the most vital role in trying to guarantee the effectiveness of citizens' constitutional rights. There have clearly been times when the Court has been ineffective in guaranteeing these rights. Examples would include:

- The Court's 1857 decision in *Dred Scott* v. *Sandford*, which stated that blacks could not become citizens of the United States and therefore were not entitled to the rights of citizenship.
- The Court's 1896 decision in *Plessy* v. *Ferguson*, which upheld segregation of the races on public transport — and by implication in other areas of public life — on the basis of 'separate but equal'.

On pp. 102–104, we shall see numerous modern-day examples of the Court upholding constitutional rights, such as:

- abortion rights for women (*Roe* v. *Wade*)
- rights of arrested persons (*Gideon* v. *Wainwright* and *Miranda* v. *Arizona*)
- rights of racial minorities (*Brown* v. *Board of Education of Topeka*)
- gun rights (*District of Columbia* v. *Heller*)

There are, however, two sides to this. Some would say, for example, that by guaranteeing abortion rights for women (*Roe* v. *Wade*), the Court failed to protect the rights of the unborn child; that by interpreting the 2nd Amendment to guarantee an individual's right to own guns (*District of Columbia* v. *Heller*), the Court failed to protect other citizens from gun crime and violence; that by upholding the so-called 'separation of church and state' and banning prayers in public schools, the Court failed to uphold citizens' 1st Amendment right to 'the free exercise' of religion.

Yet another line of argument would be that, having once safeguarded a right, the Court may at a later date back-track on this. The following examples come to mind:

- the Court's 2003 decision in *Gratz* v. *Bollinger*, which declared the University of Michigan's affirmative action-based admissions programme to be unconstitutional
- the Court's 2007 decision in *Gonzales* v. *Carhart*, which banned a certain abortion procedure, having upheld it in 2000

Now test yourself

26 What are constitutional rights?
27 What is the role of Congress in facilitating these rights?
28 What is the role of the executive branch in facilitating these rights?
29 Give an example of where the Supreme Court did not safeguard a constitutional right.
30 Give an example of where the Supreme Court has safeguarded a constitutional right.
31 Give an example of where the Supreme Court has back-tracked on a constitutional right.

Answers on pp. 109–110

Tested

Exam practice

A Short answer questions:
   1 Explain how the checks and balances between the president and Congress work. [15]
   2 How and why is federalism enshrined in the Constitution? [15]
   3 How are constitutional rights protected? [15]

B Essay questions:
   1 Why is the federal government better described as one of 'shared powers' rather than 'separation of powers'? [45]
   2 Why has the Constitution been subject to so few amendments? [45]
   3 How and why has federalism evolved? [45]

Answers and quick quiz 5 online

Online

6 Congress

The structure of Congress

Congress is the overall name for both houses. Congress is made up of two houses — the House of Representatives and the Senate. Congress is therefore described as **bicameral**.

> **Bicameral** means made up of two houses or chambers.

In the House of Representatives there are 435 members. Each state has a certain number of members proportional to the population of the state. Except in states that have just one House member, each member represents a sub-division of the state known as a 'District'. By the time of the 2012 elections, California (the largest state) had 53, Wyoming (the smallest state) just one. As we have already seen (p. 24), members are elected for 2-year terms and the Constitution states that to be a member of the House of Representatives you must:

- be at least 25 years of age
- have been a US citizen for at least 7 years
- be a resident of the state in which your District is situated

In the House of Representatives at the beginning of the 112th Congress (January 2011), among the 435 members there were:

- 72 women
- 42 African-Americans
- 26 Hispanics
- no ex-senators

Examiner's tip

There is potential confusion in the terms used to refer to members of each house. The problem lies in the fact that, although the term 'Congress' refers to both houses, the term 'Congressman' refers only to members of the House of Representatives. Members of the Senate are called 'Senators'.

As Table 6.1 shows, the number of women and African-American members in the House has increased quite significantly over the past 30 years. This was particularly the case following the elections in 1992. But the 72 women members at the start of the 112th Congress (2011–12) still represent only 16% of the membership, well below the percentage they make up of the US electorate. For African-Americans, the 42 members represent 9%, only slightly below their 10% in society as a whole. This tells us something about how representative Congress is.

Table 6.1 Women and African-American members of the House and Senate since 1991

| Years | House of Representatives | | Senate | |
	Women	African-Americans	Women	African-Americans
1991–92	28	25	2	0
1993–94	47	38	7	1
1995–96	48	38	8	1
1997–98	51	38	9	1
1999–2000	56	35	9	0
2001–02	59	36	13	0
2003–04	59	38	14	0
2005–06	64	41	14	1
2007–08	71	40	16	1
2009–10	75	39	17	1
2011–12	72	42	17	0

Senate membership

Revised

In the Senate there are 100 members. Each state — regardless of population — has two senators. Each senator represents the entire state. They are elected for 6-year terms. One-third of the Senate is up for re-election every 2 years. Senate elections are held on the same day as elections to the House.

The Constitution states that to be a senator you must:

● be at least 30 years of age
● have been a US citizen for at least 9 years
● be a resident of the state you represent

In the Senate at the beginning of the 112th Congress (January 2011), among the 100 members there were:

● 17 women
● no African-Americans
● 2 Hispanics
● 50 ex-House members

Again, as in the House, the number of women members has increased of late but still stands at a proportionately low number (see Table 6.1). Following the defeat of Democrat Carol Moseley Braun of Illinois in 1998, there were no African-American senators until the election of Barack Obama in 2004, who served until his election as president in 2008. Following the 2010 mid-term elections, there were no African-Americans in the Senate. It is highly significant that half of the current Senate are former members of the House of Representatives. This is an important indicator of the perceived power and prestige of the Senate in comparison to the House.

Now test yourself

1 How many houses make up Congress?

2 How many members are there in each?

3 How is the membership of each house distributed among the 50 states?

4 How many women and African-Americans are there in each house?

5 What has happened to the numbers of these two groups in Congress over the past 30 years?

Tested

The powers of Congress

In terms of powers, each house has **exclusive powers** and **joint powers**. In other words, each house has powers that it alone — and not the other house — possesses. Equally, each house shares powers with the other house.

Exclusive powers

Revised

The House of Representatives has three exclusive powers:

1 to begin consideration of all money bills
2 to **impeach** any member of the executive or judicial branches of the federal government
3 to elect the president if the Electoral College is deadlocked

The Founding Fathers gave the House of Representatives the power to begin consideration of all money bills because it was the only directly elected chamber at that time.

In 1998, the House of Representatives impeached President Clinton on two counts — perjury and obstruction of justice. Clinton was then the seventeenth person to be impeached by the House since the first case in 1797, but only the second president. President Andrew Johnson was impeached — and acquitted by the Senate — in 1868. Other than two presidents, those impeached have included:

● one senator
● one Cabinet member
● one Supreme Court justice
● 14 other federal judges (trial and appeal courts)

The third power — to elect the president if the Electoral College is deadlocked — is now almost redundant, not having been used since 1824.

The Senate has four exclusive powers:

1 to ratify all treaties negotiated by the president — a two-thirds majority required
2 to confirm many appointments (to the executive and judicial branches) made by the president — a simple majority required
3 to try cases of impeachment — a two-thirds majority required to convict and remove from office
4 to elect the vice-president if the Electoral College is deadlocked

It is the first two of these exclusive powers that go some way to making the Senate the more powerful and prestigious of the two chambers.

Only the Senate has the power to ratify treaties and confirm appointments. Although the Senate usually agrees, remember that presidents will generally only submit those treaties and appointments that they know the Senate will approve. Thus the Senate has a kind of hidden power. In 1999, the Senate rejected the Comprehensive Test Ban Treaty. The vote was 48–51, 18 votes short of the two-thirds majority required.

Typical mistakes

The term 'impeachment' is often misunderstood. It simply means to make a formal accusation or to bring charges against someone. It does not mean to remove someone from office, though it may lead to that.

Examiner's tip

Be really up-to-date and try to include Judge Thomas Porteous, who was impeached, tried and removed from office in 2010 by a vote in the Senate of 94–2, well over the required two-thirds majority.

The same year, the Senate rejected President Clinton's nomination of Ronnie White to be a judge of the federal trial court. The vote here was 45–54, 5 votes short of the simple majority required.

Once the House has impeached someone, the Senate tries that case of impeachment. To find the person guilty, two-thirds of the senators voting must vote 'guilty'. In the votes on the two charges brought against President Clinton, the Senate voted 45–55 and 50–50, respectively 22 and 17 votes short of the two-thirds majority required.

The final exclusive Senate power — to elect the vice-president if the Electoral College is deadlocked — remains unused since 1824.

> **Typical mistakes**
>
> Because Clinton was found not guilty and therefore remained in office, many wrongly think he was therefore not impeached. He was impeached, but found not guilty of the charges.

Joint powers

Revised

Together, the House of Representatives and the Senate have five joint powers:

1 to pass legislation, including the budget

2 to conduct investigations regarding the actions of the executive branch

3 to initiate constitutional amendments

4 to declare war

5 to confirm a newly appointed vice-president

> **Typical mistakes**
>
> Notice that they confirm only a newly *appointed* vice-president, not one who is *elected*.

It is important to remember that the House and the Senate share arguably the most important power of Congress, that of passing legislation. Unlike in the UK Parliament, where the House of Commons dominates the legislative process, in the US Congress the two chambers have equal legislative power. This can be seen in the following ways:

● All legislation must pass through all stages in both houses.

● Both houses conduct detailed scrutiny of legislation in committee.

● Both houses have full power of amendment over all bills, usually resulting in there being two different versions of the same bill once it has gone through both houses.

● Conference committees — set up to reconcile the two different versions of the same bill — are made up of members of both houses and their decisions must be agreed to by both houses.

● It takes a two-thirds majority in both houses to override a presidential veto.

Both houses have standing committees, which can conduct investigations of the work of the executive branch. Both houses can also establish select committees to perform the same function.

In order to propose an amendment to the Constitution, a two-thirds majority is required in both houses (see p. 61).

The joint power to declare war has become somewhat redundant. The power has not been used since December 1941, when Congress declared war on Japan following the attack on Pearl Harbor. That was the fifth time it had been used, the others being:

● the war of 1812 (against Great Britain)

● the Mexican war in 1846

- the Spanish–American war in 1898
- the First World War in 1917

The final joint power is relatively new, having been granted in 1967 by the 25th Amendment. Should the office of the vice-presidency become vacant between elections, the president is now empowered to nominate a new vice-president to fill the vacancy. But the nomination must be confirmed by a simple majority vote in both houses of Congress.

The power has been used twice. In 1973, Vice-President Spiro Agnew resigned shortly before pleading 'no contest' to a charge of income tax evasion. President Nixon appointed Congressman Gerald Ford as his new vice-president. Ford was confirmed by the Senate by 92 votes to 3, and by the House 387–35. Less than a year later, Nixon resigned and Ford became president, again leaving the vice-presidency vacant. Ford chose former New York Governor Nelson Rockefeller, who was easily confirmed in the Senate (90–7) but by 287-128 in the House.

Now test yourself

Tested

6 What are the three exclusive powers of the House?
7 What does the term 'impeachment' mean?
8 What are the four exclusive powers of the Senate?
9 What majorities are required to (a) ratify a treaty and (b) convict someone in an impeachment trial?
10 What are the five joint powers of Congress?
11 What majority is required to propose a constitutional amendment in Congress?
12 How many times has Congress declared war and when was the last time?

Comparison between the House and the Senate

Revised

Having looked at the membership and powers of both houses, let us compare the two houses. This tells us about the distribution of power within Congress. It is often suggested that the Senate is more powerful and prestigious than the House. Is this the case? There is a 'yes' and a 'no' answer.

Reasons why the Senate is often thought of as being more prestigious and powerful than the House of Representatives are:

- Senators represent the entire state, not just part of the state.
- Senators serve 6-year terms, three times as long as House members.
- As a senator you are one of 100, rather than one of 435.
- Senators are therefore likely to chair a committee much sooner in their career than their House counterparts.
- Senators often enjoy greater name recognition, not only in their state but often across the nation as a whole.
- House members frequently seek election to the Senate; the reverse is almost unknown.
- Senators are more frequently thought of as likely presidential candidates. Recent examples are senators Barack Obama (D), Hillary Clinton (D) and John McCain (R), all of whom contested their party's presidential nomination race in 2008.

Examiner's tip

This has been a frequent focus for A-level questions. Too many candidates forget to argue the 'no' side. Although in some important ways the Senate is more powerful than the House, in some important functions the House is of equal importance.

- Senators are more frequently nominated as vice-presidential running-mates. Recent examples are Senators Joe Lieberman (2000), John Edwards (2004) and Joe Biden (2008) — all Democrats.
- Senators have exclusive powers, including the ratification of treaties and the confirmation of appointments, which are generally agreed to be more significant than the exclusive powers enjoyed by House members.

However, it is also important to remember that in some ways Senate and House members are equal. The most important argument here concerns the equality of the two houses in the legislative process:

- All bills must go through all stages in both houses; neither can overturn the decisions of the other.
- Both houses have powerful standing committees that conduct separate hearings at the committee stage.
- At the conference committee stage, members of both houses are represented (see p. 73).
- Both houses must agree to the compromise reached at the conference committee.
- To override a presidential veto, a two-thirds majority in both houses is required.

(see p. 73).

Examiner's tip

To help you with questions that ask you to examine the claim that the Senate is more powerful and prestigious than the House, construct a two-column table, putting arguments for on one side and arguments against on the other.

Now test yourself

13 How many ex-members of the other house are there in (a) the Senate and (b) the House?

14 Who is presiding officer of (a) the Senate and (b) the House?

Tested ☐

Debate

Comparison between Senate and House

Table 6.2 Senate and House compared

	Senate	House
Number of members	100	435
Number per state	2	Proportional to population
Length of term	6 years	2 years
Age qualification	30	25
Citizenship qualification	9 years	7 years
Average age	62	56
Presiding officer	Vice-president	Speaker
Number of women	17	72
Number of African-Americans	0	42
Ex-members of other house	50	0
Special powers	• Ratify treaties • Confirm appointments • Try cases of impeachment • Elect vice-president if Electoral College is deadlocked	• Initiate money bills • Impeachment • Elect president if Electoral College is deadlocked
Joint powers	• Legislation • Declare war • Initiate constitutional amendments • Confirm newly appointed vice-president	

Distribution of power in Congress

Power in Congress is mainly distributed between two groups of people: the party leadership and committee chairs. The main party leadership posts in Congress are:

- the Speaker of the House of Representatives
- the Majority and Minority Leaders of both houses
- standing committee chairmen

Speaker of the House of Representatives   Revised

The Speaker of the House of Representatives is:

- elected by the entire House membership at the beginning of each new Congress (i.e. every 2 years)
- usually the nominee of the majority party in the House at the time
- not required by the Constitution to be a serving member of the House, though all Speakers have been
- next in line to the presidency after the vice-president, but this is less significant with the passage of the 25th Amendment requiring the vice-presidency to be filled if a vacancy should occur there

Unlike the Speaker of the House of Commons, the Speaker of the House of Representatives is a party political player. In essence, the Speaker is the leader of the majority party in the House and, if of a different party from the president, may act as the major spokesperson for the party, a kind of 'leader of the opposition'.

The Speaker has the following powers and functions:

- acts as the presiding officer of the House (i.e. chairs debates)
- interprets and enforces the rules of the House, and decides points of order
- refers bills to committees
- appoints select and conference committee chairs
- appoints majority party members of the House Rules Committee (see p. 72)
- may exercise considerable influence in the flow of legislation through the House, as well as in committee assignments for majority party members and even the selection of House standing committee chairs

Some Speakers have become politicians of considerable stature and importance. Recent examples are Democrat Nancy Pelosi and Republican Newt Gingrich. Others, such as Dennis Hastert, have been more low-key.

Majority and Minority Leaders   Revised

In both the House and the Senate, there is a Majority and a Minority Leader. They are elected by their respective party groups in each house every 2 years at the start of each Congress.

Exam practice answers and quick quizzes at **www.therevisionbutton.co.uk/myrevisionnotes**

In both houses, the Majority and Minority Leaders:

- act as day-by-day 'directors of operations' on the floor of their respective houses
- hold press briefings to talk about their party's policy agenda
- act as liaison between the House/Senate and the White House

In the Senate, they make unanimous consent agreements to bring bills for debate on the Senate floor (see p. 75).

In the House, the Majority Leader plays a 'number two' role to the Speaker. The Majority and Minority Leaders may hope to become Speaker. Most Speakers — though not Dennis Hastert — previously held one of these two posts.

The other place where power resides in Congress is in the committee chairs, as we shall see in the next section.

Now test yourself

15 Name three leadership posts in Congress.

16 What are the powers of the House Speaker?

Tested

The committee system

Power in Congress is also identified with the **committee system**. There are many different types of committee in both houses of Congress. The most important are:

- standing committees
- the House Rules Committee
- conference committees

> The **committee system** of Congress is made up of different types of committee which perform legislative and investigatory functions.

Standing committees

Revised

Membership

Standing committees exist in both houses of Congress. Here's what you need to know about standing committees:

- They are permanent (that is what 'standing' means), policy specialist committees.
- There are 16 in the Senate and 17 in the House.
- Plus, in the House, there is the House Rules Committee (see p. 72).
- Most of them have subcommittees.
- Typical size is around 18 members in the Senate committees and around 45–50 in House committees.
- The party balance in each committee is in the same proportion as that which exists within the chamber as a whole.
- Chairmen are always drawn from the chamber's majority party.
- Most chairmen, especially in the Senate, are chosen through the **seniority rule**.

Typical mistakes

Do make sure you can spell the word 'committee' – two 'm's, two 't's and two 'e's.

> The **seniority rule** states that the chairman of a standing committee will be the member of the majority party with the longest continuous service on that committee.

Typical mistakes

Make sure you get this definition exactly right. The word 'continuous' is important.

Functions

House standing committees have two functions. Senate standing committees have the same two plus another. These functions are as follows:

1 To conduct the committee stage of the legislative process.

2 To conduct investigations within the committee's policy area. This fulfils Congress's role of oversight.

This function is not specifically granted by the Constitution but is an implied power. Members of Congress have to know what is going on in order to make the laws, as well as to see how the laws they have passed are working.

It is important to remember when dealing with Congress's oversight function that:

- the executive is physically separated from the legislature
- members of Congress elected to the executive (e.g. Obama and Biden in 2008) must resign from Congress
- questioning of executive branch members occurs in the committee rooms, not on the floor of the chambers
- the effectiveness of this oversight is open to question, especially when the presidency and Congress are controlled by the same party (e.g. 2009–10)
- some think that oversight is more effective when party control is divided (e.g. 2007–08)

3 (*In the Senate only*) To begin the confirmation process of numerous presidential appointments to both the executive and judicial branches of the federal government.

To fulfil these functions, standing committees hold hearings attended by witnesses. At the conclusion of hearings — which may last anything from a few hours to a day, to a week, or a month or more — votes will be taken to recommend action to the full chamber.

House Rules Committee

Revised

Officially this is one of the standing committees of the House, but it performs such a distinctive function that it is better dealt with separately.

Nearly all bills pass through the House Rules Committee. It has the following functions:

- It timetables bills for consideration on the floor of the House.
- It deals with getting bills from the committee stage to the second reading.
- It prioritises the most important bills, giving them quick passage to the House floor.
- It gives a 'Rule' to each bill passing on to the floor for its second reading. The 'Rule' sets out the rules of debate by stating, for example, what, if any, amendments can be made to the bill at this stage.

For these reasons, the House Rules Committee is potentially an important committee.

Examiner's tip

A 'Rule' is best thought of as a kind of admission ticket to the House floor. It is what you need to go on to the next stage (i.e. the second reading on the House floor).

Conference committees

Conference committees are required because of two important characteristics about the legislative process in the US Congress:

1 Both houses have equal power.

2 Bills pass through both houses at the same time.

As a consequence, there are two different versions of each bill — a House version and a Senate version. And by the time the bill has passed through each house, the two versions are likely to be very different. If after the third reading in each house the two versions of the bill are different, and if these differences cannot be sorted out informally, then a conference committee is likely to be set up.

Conference committees (whose members are referred to as 'conferees'):

● are ad hoc (i.e. temporary) — set up to consider a particular bill and then disbanded

● contain members of both houses

● have one function — to reconcile the differences between the two versions of the same bill

When the conference committee has come up with an agreed version of the bill, this must be agreed to by a vote on the floor of each house. There has been a significant decline in the use of conference committees since 1995. Both parties when in the majority have often resorted to a more ad hoc, leadership-driven approach, where one chamber is simply asked to endorse the legislation passed by the other chamber in a system not dissimilar to what occurs in the UK Parliament. This is what happened with the healthcare reform bill in 2010.

Now test yourself

17 Name three different types of committee.

18 How many members typically make up standing committees in each house?

19 How is the party balance of each standing committee decided?

20 What is the seniority rule?

21 What functions do standing committees have?

22 Where does the questioning of executive branch members in Congress occur?

23 Explain why this has to be the case.

24 What does the House Rules Committee do?

25 What is the function of a conference committee?

The legislative process

Overview

In this section we find out more about the structure and workings of Congress as well as its representative function and the relationship between Congress and the presidency.

When studying the legislative process in Congress, it is also important to remember the following points:

- Both houses have equal power when dealing with legislation.
- Bills pass through the House and Senate concurrently.
- A 'Congress' lasts for 2 years.
- Any bills not completed in one Congress must start the process again at the beginning in the next Congress.
- A huge number of bills — around 10,000–14,000 — are introduced during a Congress.
- Only a small proportion of these — 400–50 bills, or 3–4% —will be successfully passed into law.
- The process is difficult and complicated.
- Supporters of a bill must win at every stage, while opponents have only to win at one stage to defeat a bill.
- There is little in the way of party discipline in Congress, which increases the difficulties.
- The president is unlikely to have his own party in control of both houses of Congress.
- It is even possible that the House and the Senate may be controlled by different parties, as from January 2011, with the Democrats controlling the Senate and the Republicans controlling the House.

The legislative process in the US Congress is best thought of in seven stages, which we will now consider.

First reading
Revised ☐

- All 'money bills' must be introduced into the House first.
- There is no debate and no vote; it is just the formality of introducing the bill.
- Bills are then immediately sent on to the committee stage.

Committee stage
Revised ☐

- Bills are referred to one of the permanent, policy specialist standing committees (see p. 71).
- It is important to note that the committee stage comes before the second reading.
- Committees have full power of amendment.
- Because of huge numbers of bills being referred to each committee, many bills are **pigeon-holed** — that is, merely put to one side and never considered.
- For a bill that is to be considered, a hearing is held with witnesses appearing before the committee.
- Hearings may be conducted either in the full committee or in subcommittee.
- Hearings can last from hours to days, weeks or even months, depending on the length of the bill and whether or not it is controversial.

Examiner's tip

It is worth remembering that whereas in Congress the committee stage comes before the second reading, in the UK Parliament the committee stage comes after the second reading. This means that the committee stage in Congress is much more important, as it comes before the whole chamber has debated the bill.

Exam practice answers and quick quizzes at **www.therevisionbutton.co.uk/myrevisionnotes**

- Once the hearings have been completed, the committee holds a **mark-up** session — making the changes it wishes — before **reporting out** the bill, effectively sending it on to its next stage.

The committee stage of a bill is of the utmost importance because:

- the committee members are regarded as policy specialists, so others look to the committee for a lead
- it is as far as most bills get
- committees have full power of amendment
- committees really do have life-and-death power over bills

Timetabling

Revised

By the time Congress has been in session for a few months, a huge number of bills will be waiting to come to the floor of the House and the Senate for their second reading. While there are dozens of committee and subcommittee rooms in each house, there is only one floor in each chamber. There develops something of a legislative traffic jam, with bills queuing for their turn on the House and Senate floors. Each house has a procedure for dealing with this potential problem.

The House of Representatives deals with this through the House Rules Committee (see p. 72). The Senate deals with it through what are called **unanimous consent agreements**. These, in effect, are agreements between the Senate Majority and Minority Leaders (see pp. 70–71) on the order in which bills will be debated on the Senate floor.

Second reading

Revised

- This is the first opportunity for most members to debate the bill.
- In the House, most bills are debated in the Committee of the Whole House, allowing for different rules of debate.
- In the Senate, bills can be subject to a **filibuster**. A filibuster can be ended by a 'closure' (or 'cloture') motion, which must be approved by three-fifths of the entire Senate (i.e. 60 senators).
- In both houses, further amendments can usually be made.
- Votes are taken on amendments — simple majorities are required to pass.
- At the end of the debate, a vote is taken on the bill.
- The vote will be either a voice vote (for non-controversial bills) or a recorded vote, in which a record of each member's vote is made.
- A simple majority is required to pass the bill.

> A **filibuster** is a delaying tactic based on the right of senators to unlimited debate. Its main purpose is to delay or defeat a bill or nomination.

Typical mistakes

It is easy to make filibusters sound as if they are silly and frivolous. Some can be. But the filibuster is an important safeguard of the interest of minorities in the Senate. And don't forget, one of the reasons the states were given equal representation in the Senate was to safeguard the interest of minorities — the smaller states.

Third reading

Revised

- This is a final opportunity to debate the bill.
- If substantial amendments were made at the second reading, the third reading is likely to occur some weeks or months after the second reading and to require another substantive debate.

- If few amendments were made at the second reading, or these amendments were approved by large majorities, the third reading may follow on almost immediately after the second reading and be a brief debate.
- At the end of the debate, another vote is taken.

Conference committee

- This is an optional stage.
- If the House version and the Senate version of the bill are the same, there is no need for a conference committee.
- If differences in the two versions of the bill can be sorted out amicably between the two houses, there is no need for a conference committee.
- If there are substantial differences between the two versions of the bill and these cannot be sorted out amicably, then a conference committee may be used (see p. 67).
- Members of the conference committee are drawn from both houses.
- Members are called conferees.

Presidential action

A bill can be passed to the president once the House and Senate have agreed on a single version of the bill.

The president always has three options:

1 *Sign the bill into law*: this he will do to bills he fully supports, and wants to be associated with and take credit for; he must sign the bill within ten congressional working days of receiving it.

2 *Leave the bill on his desk*: this he will do to bills he only partly supports, those he takes no position on at all, or those he would wish to veto but has decided not to. These bills will become law without his signature within ten congressional working days.

3 *Veto the bill*: this he will do to bills he clearly opposes. A **presidential veto** must be used within ten congressional working days of receiving the bill by sending it back to its house of origin with a note explaining his objections. To override the veto, the bill must be passed by a two-thirds majority in both houses. This is difficult to achieve. Congress managed to override only two of Bill Clinton's 36 regular vetoes in 8 years. However, they overrode four of George W. Bush's 11 regular vetoes in his 8 years. (For more detail, see pp. 83–84.)

At the end of a congressional session, the president has a fourth option:

4 *Pocket-veto the bill*: if, while the bill is awaiting the president's action, the congressional session ends, the bill is lost. This is called a **pocket veto** and it cannot be overridden by Congress.

For about a year during the Clinton presidency, the president had a fifth option — **the line-item veto**. This allowed him to sign parts of a bill into law while vetoing other parts to do with spending. But in 1998, the Supreme Court declared the power unconstitutional. During the brief time that President Clinton had the power, he used it on 11 bills.

> **Typical mistakes**
>
> Some candidates misuse the word 'veto'. They say that if Congress defeats a bill, Congress has 'vetoed' the bill. Congress cannot 'veto' a bill; only the president can do that.

> The **presidential veto** is a power vested in the president by which he can return a bill to Congress unsigned.

> **Now test yourself**
>
> 26 Why is the committee stage of a bill so important?
>
> 27 What is a filibuster?
>
> 28 What options does the president have when a bill is sent to him?
>
> 29 What is a presidential veto?
>
> 30 How can Congress override a veto?
>
> Tested

Voting in Congress: party and representation

In this section, we are going to consider, among other things, more about the relationship between the Congress and the presidency as well the significance of parties in Congress.

House and Senate members are called upon to cast a large number of votes each year — in 2010, 664 recorded votes in the House and 299 in the Senate. What factors make them vote as they do? In the UK House of Commons, the answer would be quite simple — party. But in the US Congress, political parties are only one of a number of factors that determine the way members vote.

One should consider the four most important determinants of voting:

1 political party
2 constituents
3 the administration
4 pressure groups

The relative importance of these determinants will vary from one politician to another and from one vote to another.

Political party
Revised

Political party is one of a number of determinants of voting in Congress. For some members, on some issues, it may be the most important determinant. But it is by no means the all-important determinant that it is for MPs in the UK House of Commons.

There are five important reasons for this difference:

1 Political parties in the USA are less centralised and ideologically cohesive than their UK counterparts.
2 US political parties do not have the 'sticks' and 'carrots' that their UK counterparts have as incentives to party unity — 'sticks' such as threats of de-selection or 'carrots' such as much sought-after jobs in the executive branch.
3 Constituents control the selection of candidates — through congressional primaries — so House and Senate members have to be far more mindful of constituents' views than of the party view.
4 House members are subject to elections every 2 years, increasing their reliance on the views of their constituents.
5 The executive branch does not depend for its existence on getting its policies through the legislature, as it does in the UK.

It is also important to realise what political commentators mean in the USA by a **party vote** in the legislature. In the UK House of Commons, a party vote would mean all the MPs on the government side of the House voting against all the MPs on the opposition side. A huge number of votes in the UK House of Commons would fit that description. But in the US Congress, when we talk of a party vote, we mean one in which the majority of one party votes 'yes' while the majority of the other party votes 'no'.

Take the example of a vote in the House on 14 April 2011 to pass the 2011 budget compromise:

- It passed by 260–167.
- Republicans voted 179 yes; 59 no.
- Democrats voted 81 yes; 108 no.
- The majority of Republicans voted 'yes'.
- The majority of Democrats voted 'no'.

Therefore this would classify as a 'party vote', despite the fact that 59 Republicans voted 'no' and 81 Democrats voted 'yes'. Despite this low threshold, in recent years only around 50–60% of votes in each chamber have been party votes.

A more typical vote in the House or the Senate is one in which the majority of members of both parties vote the same way. Take, for example, a vote in the House on 16 December 2010 on the Tax Relief, Unemployment Insurance and Job Creation Act:

- It passed by 277–148.
- Democrats voted 139–112.
- Republicans voted 138–36.

Constituents

Revised

In looking at the role of constituents in voting, we are considering the adequacy of Congress's representative role. Why then do House and Senate members place the views of their constituents so highly in their voting priorities?

There are four reasons to consider:

1 The Constitution states that House and Senate members must be residents of the state they represent, so this gives them a good understanding of what 'the folks back home' are saying.

2 Some states go further by insisting that House members reside in the actual district (constituency) they represent.

3 Many House and Senate members will have been born and educated, lived and worked in the state/district they now represent.

4 House members are especially careful about constituents' views because they have to face election every 2 years.

> **Examiner's tip**
> This is known as the 'locality rule'.

How do House and Senate members find out what their constituents want while they are working in Washington DC? There are various methods, which include:

- visits from constituents
- phone calls, letters, faxes and e-mails from constituents
- keeping in constant touch with their offices back in the state/district
- reading the newspapers published in their state/district

But they will also discover what their constituents want by making frequent visits back to their state/district. The frequency will depend on how far this is from Washington DC. Once back in their state/district, House and Senate members will:

- hold party and 'town hall' meetings
- conduct 'surgeries' with individual constituents
- make visits around the state/district
- appear on local radio phone-in programmes
- be interviewed by representatives of the local media
- address various groups, such as chambers of commerce, professional groups and Round Table lunches
- visit local schools, hospitals and businesses

All these will help them keep in touch with their constituents and thus with fulfilling their role of **representation**.

However, when it comes to voting, three further factors must be remembered:

1 Except on some exceptional issues, local opinion is likely to be divided, with some in favour and some against.
2 Through constituency mail and visits, the House/Senate member is more likely to hear from the discontented than the contented.
3 A member of Congress is meant to be more than just a mere 'delegate' of their constituents and may need to balance other factors, as well as the national good, against what is perceived as being merely locally popular.

> **Representation** has two distinct meanings: (1) how legislators represent the views of their constituents; (2) how representative legislators are of society as a whole in such matters as race and gender.

> **Typical mistake**
>
> This is important. Candidates too often talk of constituency interest as if on all issues everyone in the state or district thinks the same way. Would that it were that simple!

The administration   Revised ☐

The term 'administration' means members of the executive branch, including the president and members of his cabinet. They are involved in the passage of legislation in a number of ways, including:

- initiating legislation
- making contact with members of Congress via phone calls, visits, etc.
- making contact with senior members of the congressional staff, including committee staff

Often, the White House itself gets involved. This will be done either by the Congressional Liaison Office or directly by the president himself trying to persuade members of Congress to support his legislation, nominations and treaties. Such persuasion needs to be:

- regular
- a two-way street (offering help, favours and cooperation in return)
- bipartisan (i.e. of two parties)

For an administration to talk only with members of their party is usually a recipe for disaster. Things tend to happen in Congress when they are supported by a bipartisan coalition.

Pressure groups

Revised

Pressure groups use a number of methods to influence the way members of Congress vote. These include:

- making contact with members of Congress: phone calls, visits, etc.
- making contact with senior members of the congressional staff
- attempting to generate public support favourable to their position
- providing evidence to relevant committee hearings to support their position
- organising rallies and demonstrations — both in Washington DC and around the country
- organising petition drives, e-mail campaigns, etc.
- money raising to fund politicians who support their cause and to seek to defeat those who do not

Certain policy areas have seen significant pressure group activity, including the environment, abortion, gun control, healthcare, welfare reform and international trade (see p. 40).

Now test yourself

Tested

31 Why are parties in Congress less important than parties in the UK House of Commons?

32 What is a party vote in Congress?

33 Give four reasons why constituents' views are so important.

34 Give the two meanings of the word 'representation'.

35 How do members of the executive branch get involved in the passage of legislation in Congress?

36 Give four ways in which pressure groups try to influence the way members of Congress vote.

Is Congress effective?

Gridlock

Revised

Finally, we need to consider the institutional effectiveness of Congress. The widespread belief is that Congress is largely ineffective. In a Gallup Poll in January 2011, a mere 20% said they approved of the job Congress was doing with 73% disapproving, feeling that Congress is often beset by **gridlock** and that little of substance is actually achieved.

> **Gridlock** is the failure to get action on policy proposals and legislation in Congress.

We have already mentioned a number of factors that cause gridlock. Let's list them:

- a complicated and lengthy legislative process in which those who want to pass bills must win at every stage
- divided government — one party controlling Congress while the other party controls the presidency
- divided Congress — one party controlling the House while the other party controls the Senate
- the use of the filibuster in the Senate

- the need for super-majorities (i.e. two-thirds, three-fifths) in certain instances
- the lack of strict party discipline
- 2-year terms of office for the House, which give a very short time frame for getting things done

Examiner's tip

To help you with questions that ask you for arguments for and against Congress being effective, construct a two-column table, putting arguments for on one side and arguments against on the other.

Ineffectiveness and scandals

Revised

Examples of Congress's ineffectiveness are:

- the recent over-politicisation of the Senate's confirmation of Supreme Court justices
- the lack of effective oversight of the executive branch under united government

And then there have been the frequent scandals that have beset Congress — whether collective (e.g. the House Bank scandal in the 1990s) or individual (sexual, financial, etc.). All this provides an impression of ineffectiveness. But in Congress's defence, the system was designed by the Founding Fathers to provide limited government. The intricate system of checks and balances was a deliberate attempt to keep government from becoming, as it were, too effective. For every critic saying that Congress does not achieve anything, there is another claiming it is doing too much.

Now test yourself

37 What evidence is there that Congress is unpopular among Americans?

38 Explain the term 'gridlock'.

39 What are the factors that may cause gridlock in Congress?

40 Why might gridlock not be a bad thing?

Answers on pp. 110–111

Tested

Exam practice

A Short answer questions:

1 Why do many members of the House of Representatives try to become senators? [15]

2 In what ways is it true to say that Congress's two houses are equal? [15]

3 What makes congressional standing committees so important? [15]

4 How important are political parties in Congress? [15]

B Essay questions:

1 To what extent is Congress still a powerful body? [45]

2 Why is it so hard to pass legislation through Congress? [45]

3 How do members of Congress decide how to vote? [45]

4 Is Congress an effective body? [45]

Answers and quick quiz 6 online

Online

7 The presidency

The powers of the president

The powers of the president are his tasks, functions or duties. They are laid out in Article II of the Constitution. These powers have been held by George Washington and Barack Obama, and all the 41 presidents between. They are the *formal* sources of presidential power.

The president has the following powers:

- to propose legislation to Congress
- to submit the annual budget to Congress
- to sign legislation passed by Congress
- to veto legislation passed by Congress
- to act as chief executive
- to nominate executive branch officials
- to nominate federal judges
- to act as commander-in-chief
- to negotiate treaties
- to pardon felons

> **Examiner's tip**
>
> Note that a president's term of office begins the year after the election. The election is in November, but the new president does not take over until the following January.

Table 7.1 American presidents since 1981

President	Party	Dates
Ronald Reagan	Republican	1981–89
George H. W. Bush	Republican	1989–93
Bill Clinton	Democrat	1993–2001
George W. Bush	Republican	2001–09
Barack Obama	Democrat	2009–

Propose legislation — Revised ☐

The president proposes legislation to Congress in a number of ways — most obviously through the annual **State of the Union Address**, when he addresses a joint session of Congress. This occurs each January, and it gives the president the chance to set out a legislative agenda for the coming year. But the president can propose legislation at any time by, for example, calling a press conference or making an announcement at some public event.

Some examples of presidential initiatives by President Obama are:

- healthcare reform
- Wall Street regulation reform
- credit card regulation reform

Submit the annual budget — Revised ☐

The annual federal budget is drawn up for the president by the Office of Management and Budget (see p. 91). The president then submits it to Congress. This is followed by a lengthy bargaining process between the president and Congress — especially lengthy if the president and Congress are controlled by different political parties.

Exam practice answers and quick quizzes at **www.therevisionbutton.co.uk/myrevisionnotes**

Sign legislation

Revised

Once bills have passed through a lengthy and complicated process in Congress (see pp. 73–76), they land on the president's desk. He has a number of options, but the most likely is that of signing the bill into law. He will do this with bills for which he wishes to take some credit.

Veto legislation

Revised

As well as signing bills into law, the president has the option of vetoing them. The **regular veto** is a much-used presidential weapon. Even the threat of it can be an important bargaining tool. Altogether, from George Washington (1789) through to the end of the presidency of George W. Bush (2009), presidents have used fewer than 1,500 regular vetoes, of which Congress has overridden 110, which means that presidents have been successful on vetoes 93% of the time. George W. Bush's success rate of just below 64% was the third lowest of any president.

To veto a bill, the president must:

- veto the whole bill, not just parts of it
- return the bill to the house which first considered it, within 10 working days
- include a note (called the 'veto message') explaining any objections

It is then up to Congress to decide what to do. Congress may decide to:

- do nothing — conceding that the president has won and that the bill will not become law
- attempt to override the president's veto

If Congress decides to attempt to override the president's veto then the bill must be passed by a two-thirds majority in both houses. But as we now know, this is exceedingly difficult to achieve. Presidents will often choose not to veto bills if they know that Congress will override them. To have a veto overridden by Congress is often politically damaging for the president.

Typical mistakes

It is important to say 'a two-thirds majority in both houses', not just 'a two-thirds majority'.

Table 7.2 gives two examples of George W. Bush's regular vetoes. In the first, the House voted to override the veto but failed to achieve the required two-thirds majority. With 412 House members voting, 275 votes were required to override the veto. The House vote fell 10 votes short of that. There was therefore no point in the Senate voting as the veto was sustained. In the second, both houses achieved a two-thirds majority and the President's veto was overridden — the bill became law.

Table 7.2 Examples of George W. Bush's regular vetoes

Bill	Final House vote	Final Senate vote	Vetoed by president	House vote to override veto	Senate vote to override veto	Result
Child's Health Insurance	265–142	64–30	12/12/2007	260–152	–	Sustained
Food Conservation/Energy	306–110	77–15	18/6/2008	317–109	80–14	Overridden

The president may also have the power of **pocket veto** at his disposal. But this can be used only after a session of Congress has adjourned. When Congress is in session, a bill becomes law after 10 working days if the president neither signs nor vetoes it. But when Congress has adjourned and the president does not sign the bill, the bill is lost. This is called a pocket veto. Because Congress is no longer in session, pocket vetoes cannot be overridden. George W. Bush used only one pocket veto in his 8 years in office.

Act as chief executive

The opening words of Article II of the Constitution state that: 'The executive power shall be vested in a President of the United States of America.' This makes the president the chief executive, in charge of running the executive branch of the federal government. This is a huge job and much of the day-to-day running is delegated to those who run the principal departments and agencies of the federal government.

Nominate executive branch officials

The president is given the power to nominate hundreds of officials to the executive branch of the federal government. The most important of these are the heads of the 15 executive departments such as State, Treasury and Agriculture. At the beginning of his presidency, Barack Obama nominated Hillary Clinton to be Secretary of State, Arne Duncan to be Secretary of Education and Tom Vilsack to be Secretary of Agriculture. All of these nominations were subject to confirmation by the Senate by a simple majority. Hillary Clinton was confirmed by 94 votes to 2.

> **Examiner's tip**
> The State Department is the US equivalent of the UK's Foreign Office so the Secretary of State in the USA is the equivalent of the Foreign Secretary in the UK.

Nominate federal judges

Again, this involves the president in making hundreds of appointments. Not only must he fill up vacancies on the Supreme Court, he must also do this for the federal trial and appeal courts. All judicial appointments are for life and therefore assume a special importance. The most important are those to the Supreme Court (see pp. 98–99). During his first 2 years in office, President Obama made two appointments to the Supreme Court: Sonia Sotomayor (2009) and Elena Kagan (2010). President George W. Bush made only two appointments during his entire 8-year presidency, as did President Clinton.

Act as commander-in-chief

This was a particularly significant power for the presidents in office between the 1940s and the early 1990s — from Franklin Roosevelt to George H. W. Bush. With the USA fighting in the Second World War and then taking the lead for the West in the Cold War, the president's commander-in-chief role was significant during a period that also saw the Korean War, the Vietnam War and the Gulf War, as well as the wars in Iraq and Afghanistan during the presidency of George W. Bush — to name only the principal conflicts. Arguably, in the post-Cold War era, this power is less to the fore. But crises will still occur and the power is potentially an important one. Again, the president is checked by Congress's 'power of the purse' as well as its powers to declare war and conduct investigations.

Negotiate treaties

Revised

The president's seal of office shows an eagle clutching a bundle of arrows in one claw, symbolising the commander-in-chief role, and an olive branch in the other to symbolise his peace-making role. President Obama negotiated the Strategic Arms Reduction Treaty (START) with Russia in 2010 — a major nuclear arms control agreement. Treaties must be ratified by the Senate by a two-thirds majority. The 2010 START treaty was ratified 71–26 in December 2010. In 1999, the Senate rejected President Clinton's Comprehensive Test Ban Treaty by a 48–51 vote.

Typical mistakes

The Test Ban Treaty vote was 18 votes short of the required majority, not 3. With 99 senators voting, 66 votes were required to ratify because treaties require a two-thirds majority.

Pardon

Revised

Presidents possess the power of pardon. Mostly used in uncontroversial cases, this power has occasionally been used in high-profile and controversial ones. The most notable was President Ford's 1974 pardon of former president Richard Nixon. President Clinton caused controversy when he issued 140 pardons on his last day in office in January 2001. President George W. Bush used the power sparingly, issuing only 189 in 8 years.

Now test yourself

Tested

1 What is the name of the annual speech that the president delivers to Congress in which he announces new proposals?
2 What does Congress need to do to override a president's regular veto?
3 What level of success have presidents enjoyed with their use of the veto?
4 In which article of the Constitution do we find the president's chief executive power?
5 What check is there on the president's nominations to the executive and the judiciary?
6 What checks exist on the president's power as commander-in-chief?
7 Give an example of a treaty that was ratified by the Senate and one that was rejected.
8 Whom did President Ford pardon in 1974?

The cabinet

Definition and membership

Revised

The president's cabinet is not mentioned in the Constitution. According to presidential scholar Richard Fenno, it is 'institutionalised by usage alone'. In other words, 'it's used because it's used'. **The cabinet** is an advice-giving group selected by the president to aid him in making decisions, membership of which is determined both by tradition and by presidential discretion. By tradition, it is made up of the heads of the 15 executive departments. By presidential discretion, others can be given 'cabinet rank', such as the US ambassador to the United Nations.

> **The cabinet** is the advisory group selected by the president to aid him in making decisions and coordinating the work of the federal government.

Cabinet recruitment
Revised

Unlike an incoming British prime minister, a newly elected US president does not have a 'shadow cabinet' ready and waiting to form the new administration. And, unlike in the British parliamentary system, where cabinet members are drawn from the legislature, members of the US president's cabinet cannot be currently serving members of Congress. Between 1961 and 2009, fewer than one in five cabinet officers had any previous experience in Congress. However, among Barack Obama's original 15 heads of departments in 2009, four had congressional experience, of whom three were serving members of Congress who had to resign their seats.

Members of the president's cabinet will, therefore, come from diverse backgrounds. These are likely to include:

- Congress, but these must be either former members (e.g. former House member Ray LaHood as Secretary of Transportation in the first Obama cabinet, who had just retired from the House in 2008) or those willing to resign their seats

- state governors (e.g. Governor Janet Napolitano of Arizona as Secretary of Homeland Security in 2009)

- city mayors (e.g. Clinton's Secretary of Transportation, Federico Peña, had been Mayor of Denver)

- academics (e.g. Steven Chu, Obama's Secretary of Energy, had been a professor of physics at Stanford University)

It is also likely that cabinet members will be policy specialists. Again, here are three such examples from the initial cabinet of President Barack Obama:

- Timothy Geithner (Treasury) — President of the Federal Reserve Bank of New York, 2003–09

- Arne Duncan (Education) — CEO of Chicago Public (i.e. state) Schools, 2001–09

- Shaun Donovan (Housing and Urban Development) — New York City Housing Commissioner, 2004–09

Presidents also like to balance their cabinet in terms of geographic region, race, gender, ideology and age. Incoming President Clinton in 1993 even went so far as to talk about having a cabinet that 'looked like America'. President Obama included in his first cabinet:

- a Lebanese-American (Ray LaHood)

- an African-American (Eric Holder)

- a Chinese-American (Steven Chu)

- two Japanese-Americans (Eric Shinseki and Gary Locke)

- two Hispanics (Hilda Solis and Ken Salazar)

> **Examiner's tip**
>
> Fenno's comment is a useful 'scholarly' quotation for your essays. Do try to learn a few short quotations like this one and include them, where relevant.

> **Typical mistakes**
>
> Don't use the term 'cabinet ministers'. The correct terms are 'cabinet members' or 'cabinet officers'.

This made Obama's cabinet the most ethnically diverse ever appointed.

All cabinet appointments have to be confirmed by a simple majority vote of the Senate. The last time the Senate rejected a president's cabinet appointee was in 1989, when they rejected John Tower, George H. W. Bush's nominee to head the Defense Department.

Cabinet meetings

Meetings of the president with the full cabinet tend to get a pretty bad press. Many who have attended them describe them as boring and a waste of time. Indeed, some presidents have held very few. Most presidents have held cabinet meetings only about once a month. Clinton managed only two or three a year, while at the other extreme both Carter and Reagan held 36 meetings in their first year in office. The number of meetings tends to decline as the administration wears on. There are three principal reasons for this:

1 Some of the functions of the cabinet are no longer applicable.

2 The president has increasing calls on his time, not least when he has to run for re-election. Jimmy Carter managed only six cabinet meetings in his final year in office.

3 Presidents tend to become disillusioned with their cabinet officers, often believing them to be disloyal.

Nonetheless, cabinet meetings can perform useful functions, both for the president and for cabinet members. They can enable the president to:

- engender team spirit — especially at the beginning of his administration
- look collegial and consultative
- give information to all cabinet members
- glean information from cabinet members — find out what's going on in each department
- debate policies
- present 'big picture' items such as the budget, tours, campaigns and initiatives
- check up on legislation going through Congress in which he has an interest
- see cabinet members whom he would not otherwise see

For cabinet members themselves, cabinet meetings serve:

- as get-to-know-you sessions — especially at the beginning of an administration when a number of cabinet colleagues may be total strangers
- to sort out inter-departmental disputes
- as a means of catching up with other members (before and/or after the meetings)
- as an opportunity to see the president — whom many of them would not otherwise see
- to gain them prestige back at their department, with first-hand news of what the president wants

Relations with the Executive Office of the President

Revised

It must be remembered that the principal job of cabinet officers is not to act as presidential advisors. There are good reasons why not:

- They have huge departments to run.
- They are not based in the White House.
- They have loyalties other than those to the president.

The last reason often leads to accusations of disloyalty from those whose principal function it is to act as 'all the president's men': that is, the members of the Executive Office of the President (EXOP), which includes the White House staff (see pp. 89–90). For while members of EXOP serve only the president, cabinet members must bear in mind the wishes of Congress (whose votes decide their departmental budgets) and their own departmental bureaucracy, as well as interest groups which have important links with their department. Unlike the Cabinet, members of EXOP enjoy close proximity and access to the president.

> **Examiner's tip**
>
> These three — Congress, the bureaucracy and pressure groups — are sometimes referred to as 'the iron triangle'.

Presidential scholar Richard Neustadt has written: '[An incoming president] must prepare the cabinet members against the shocking discovery that most of them are not the principal advisors to the president, are not going to be, and never will be, not since the White House staff has come into mature existence.'

The cabinet: important or unimportant?

Revised

How important is the cabinet? Individually its members are very important, though some members are far more important than others. They run huge executive departments and spend vast budgets. But collectively, the cabinet can never be that important. There are six main reasons for this:

1 Article II of the Constitution states that 'all executive power shall be vested in a President'.
2 There is no doctrine of collective responsibility.
3 The president is not 'first among equals' — he is just 'first'. As Professor Anthony King has stated: 'He doesn't sum up at the end of the meeting; he is the meeting.'
4 Cabinet officers are not his political rivals; they are not about to become president.
5 They have a problem of divided loyalty as well as a lack of proximity and access to the president.
6 The president has EXOP, which is important in helping and advising him to achieve his goals.

'The very nature of the cabinet — a body with no constitutional standing, members with no independent political base of their own and no requirement that the president seeks or follows their advice — helps contribute to its lack of influence as a collective body.' (Professor Michael Genovese)

> **Debate**
>
> Cabinet: important or unimportant?

> **Examiner's tip**
>
> In essays, it is important to make clear the distinction between the cabinet as *individuals* and the cabinet as a *collectivity*. So, for example, although in the Obama administration, certain individuals in the cabinet are very important, the cabinet as a collectivity is not all that important, and meets only about four times a year.

> **Examiner's tip**
>
> To help you with questions that ask you for arguments for and against the importance of the president's cabinet, construct a two-column table, putting arguments for on one side and arguments against on the other.

Tested

Now test yourself

9 Give a definition of the president's cabinet.

10 Why do so few cabinet members come from Congress?

11 Where else do presidents look when recruiting their cabinet?

12 What functions can cabinet meetings serve for the president?

13 What functions can cabinet meetings serve for the cabinet members?

14 Why do cabinet members make poor presidential advisors?

15 What advantages do members of EXOP have over members of the cabinet?

The Executive Office of the President

Definition and membership

Revised

The **Executive Office of the President** is an umbrella term for an organisation that consists of the top presidential staff agencies that provide help, advice, coordination and administrative support for the president.

Created in 1939, after the Brownlow Committee reported that 'the president needs help', EXOP has grown to include around a dozen or so offices. The most important ones are:

- the White House Office
- the National Security Council
- the Office of Management and Budget

Why did presidents from the mid-twentieth century 'need help' in running the federal government? The main reason was the huge increase in the size and scale of the federal government caused by nineteenth-century westward expansion and industrialisation. This was then added to by two subsidiary reasons:

- the 'New Deal' programme introduced by FDR to help cure the effects of the Depression
- the USA's newly found role as a world power

> The **Executive Office of the President** consists of the top staff agencies in the White House that give the president help and advice.

The White House Office

Revised

The White House Office includes the president's most trusted and closest aides and advisors, such as the Press Secretary, Chief of Staff and Assistant to the President for Legislative Affairs.

The principal function of those who work in the White House Office is to provide advice and administrative support for the president on a daily basis. This will involve:

- policy advice
- personnel management

- crisis management
- liaison with the federal bureaucracy
- liaison with Congress
- running the White House
- deciding and executing the president's daily schedule
- acting as 'lightning conductors' for the president
- ensuring an orderly decision-making process for the president

Members of the White House staff are meant to act not as policy-makers, but as **'honest brokers'**. They are not meant to be always in the media spotlight, but to have something of a **passion for anonymity**. As then Chief of Staff Dick Cheney stated of his relationship with President Ford: 'He takes the credit; I take the blame.'

Examiner's tip

Honest broker = an impartial adviser

Passion for anonymity = a desire to remain in the background, out of the limelight

The role of the White House Chief of Staff is the most critical. Some (e.g. 'Mack' McLarty, 1993–94) have been overwhelmed by the job, possibly because of their own lack of Washington experience. Others (e.g. John H. Sununu, 1989–92) became far too obtrusive and wanted to become a kind of 'deputy president'. The best model is that of the 'honest broker', 'salesman' and 'javelin catcher' for the president, played well by such people as Leon Panetta (Bill Clinton) and Andrew Card (George W. Bush).

The National Security Council

Revised ☐

Created in 1947, the National Security Council (NSC) was established to help the president coordinate foreign and defence policy. Headed by the National Security Advisor (NSA), the NSC began life as an in-house think-tank for the president. The NSC would gather information, advice and policy options from groups such as:

- the State Department
- the Defense Department (sometimes referred to as The Pentagon)
- the Central Intelligence Agency (CIA)
- relevant congressional committees (e.g. the Senate Foreign Relations Committee)
- the Joint Chiefs of Staff (JCS)

The NSC would then act as 'honest broker' and policy coordinator to present carefully argued options ready for presidential decision making.

President Nixon greatly increased the role of the NSA when he appointed Henry Kissinger to the post. Kissinger became a roving foreign policy-maker for the president, largely cutting out the State Department and other agencies, becoming a policy player rather than a mere facilitator. But this new enhanced role for the NSA caused grave problems for both Presidents Carter (over the Iranian hostage crisis) and Reagan (over the Iran–Contra affair). Subsequent NSAs, such as Brent Scowcroft (George H. W. Bush), Sandy Berger (Bill Clinton) and Condoleezza Rice (George W. Bush), have reverted to the more traditional role.

The Office of Management and Budget

Revised

President Nixon created the Office of Management and Budget (OMB) in 1970 when he revamped the then Bureau of the Budget.

The two principal functions of the OMB are:

1 to advise the president on the allocation of federal funds in the annual budget

2 to oversee the spending of all federal government departments and agencies

It is headed by the OMB director, just about the only EXOP post that requires Senate confirmation. Some former OMB directors, such as Leon Panetta for Bill Clinton (1993–94), have provided first-class help and advice for the president on financial and budget matters. Others have proved politically embarrassing (Reagan's David Stockman) or have led the president down disastrous paths (George H. W. Bush's Richard Darman, who in 1990 advised the President that breaking his 'no new taxes' pledge would not be politically costly in his re-election bid in 2 years' time).

Now test yourself

16 What is the Executive Office of the President (EXOP)?

17 When was EXOP created?

18 What was the main reason why was it created?

19 Name the three most important offices within EXOP.

20 Give two phrases that best describe the way the White House Chief of Staff should work.

21 What is the main function of the NSC?

22 From which other organisations is the NSC meant to gather information?

23 What are the two main functions of the OMB?

Tested

Relations with Congress

Now we turn to the relationship between the president and Congress. This section will also look at what can be called the *informal* sources of presidential power, as the president tries to persuade and bargain with members of Congress.

Checks by Congress

Revised

Almost every power that the president possesses is checked by Congress. The president, therefore, needs Congress's agreement. But in a system of 'separated institutions, sharing powers' (Richard Neustadt), this is by no means easy. And party links do not help much either. The president and the majority of Congress may be of different parties, as was the case during the last 2 years of George W. Bush's presidency (2007–08), with a Republican president but the Democrats controlling both houses of Congress.

And even when the two branches are controlled by the same party, this is no guarantee of action — witness the difficulties Bill Clinton experienced in his failed attempt to pass his healthcare reforms in 1993–94. As Neustadt has stated: 'What the Constitution separates, the political parties do not combine.'

But the president needs Congress. As Table 7.3 shows, without it he can do little or nothing. This is all part of the intricate system of 'checks and balances' devised by the Founding Fathers. Professor S. E. Finer has likened the president and Congress to 'two halves of a bank note, each useless without the other'. And the Founding Fathers' desire for cooperation and compromise ('ambition must counteract ambition', as James Madison put it) often leads to gridlock.

Examiner's tip

What the Constitution separates is, of course, the three branches of the federal government.

Typical mistakes

If you are using this quotation, do watch the spelling of the word 'separate' – it's 'a's in the middle and 'e's at either end.

Examiner's tip

What Madison meant by this was that the 'ambition' of the president (i.e. what he wants to do) must be checked by the 'ambition' of Congress (i.e. what it wants to do) and vice versa.

Table 7.3 Powers of the president and checks by Congress

Powers of the president	Checks by Congress
Propose legislation	Amend/block legislation
Submit the annual budget	Amend/block budget
Veto legislation	Override veto
Nominate executive officials (e.g. cabinet)	Senate's power of confirmation
Nominate federal judges	Senate's power of confirmation
Negotiate treaties	Senate's power of ratification
Commander-in-chief of the armed forces	Declare war/power of the purse
Act as chief executive	Investigation/impeachment/trial/removal

Examiner's tip

If you are answering a question about 'how' the president persuades/works with Congress, don't forget to begin your essay by saying why he needs to do this.

Thus, presidents cannot rely on formal powers alone to get what they want. They must also use informal powers of persuasion. As Richard Neustadt succinctly puts it: 'The president's power is the power to persuade.'

Methods of presidential persuasion

Revised

'I sit here all day trying to persuade people to do the things they ought to have sense enough to do without my persuading them…That's all the powers of the president amount to', famously commented a frustrated President Harry Truman. But Truman was right. So how does a president persuade? There are two methods — through people and through perks.

Persuasion through people

The president, if he is to be a successful persuader, must work through a number of other people. He cannot — nor should he try to — do it all himself. Whom can he use?

- *The vice-president*: as presiding officer of the Senate, he has a foothold in Congress. (All of the last six VPs have formerly been members of Congress, which also helps.)
- His own *Office of Legislative Affairs*: this is part of the White House Office and those who work here act as full-time lobbyists for the president in Congress.
- *Cabinet officers*: these work in their own policy-related area.
- *Party leaders* in Congress, including the House Speaker, Majority and Minority Leaders in both houses, whips, committee chairs and ranking minority members (see pp. 70–71).

Persuasion through perks

This works hand-in-hand with the people mentioned above.
The president may:

- make phone calls to selected members of Congress
- offer help with legislation that benefits members' constituents
- offer help with federal executive/judicial appointments of interest to constituents
- invite members to a meeting at the White House
- go to **Capitol Hill** to address a selected group of members
- offer to campaign for members of his own party

Examiner's tip

Capitol Hill, in Washington DC, is where the building housing Congress (i.e. The Capitol) stands.

If all else fails, the president can go on national television to appeal directly to the people. This is what President Johnson called 'putting Congress's feet to the fire'.

Results of presidential persuasion

Revised

David Mervin has described the president's relationship with Congress as being 'bargainer-in-chief' — and he is. But after all is said and done, the president will be hoping that it will result in his legislation being passed, his appointments confirmed and his treaties ratified.

The president's success rate is measured each year in what is called the **presidential support score**. This annual statistic measures how often the president won in roll-call votes in the House and Senate in which he took a clear position, expressed as a percentage of the whole. In 2009, President Obama had a support score of 96.7% — the highest ever recorded. In 2007, George W. Bush's support score was just 38%.

Although the presidential support score is a useful guide to presidential success, keep in mind that:

- the score does not measure the importance of votes
- presidents can avoid low scores simply by not taking positions on votes they expect to lose
- the score does not count bills which fail even to come to a vote on the floor of either house (e.g. Bill Clinton's healthcare reform bill never came to a vote in either house in 1994 and therefore did not feature in the 86% support score recorded that year)

See pp. 73–80 for further material on relations between the Congress and the presidency.

Now test yourself

Tested

24 What is the four-word phrase used by Neustadt to describe the system of government in the USA?

25 What are the checks that Congress has on the following presidential powers: (a) to propose legislation; (b) to veto legislation; (c) to nominate executive officials; (d) to nominate federal judges; (e) to negotiate treaties?

26 What checks does Congress have on the president's powers as (a) commander-in-chief and (b) chief executive?

27 Complete the following: 'The president's power is the power to _____' (one word).

28 Whom does the president use to persuade members of Congress to support his policies?

29 Give four different 'perks' that the president might use as methods of persuasion.

30 What phrase does David Mervin use to describe the president's relationship with Congress?

31 What is the presidential support score?

Relations with the Supreme Court

The president's nomination power

Revised

The president has two main powers relating to the Supreme Court. The first is a *formal* power — the power to nominate justices to the

Court when a vacancy occurs. The president may have the opportunity thereby to change the ideological balance of the nine-member Court. Justices can be thought of as being 'liberal' or 'conservative'. Those who are of a more independent nature may be described as 'moderate' or 'swing justices'. Liberal justices are likely to be appointed by Democrat presidents; conservative justices by Republican presidents. Recent examples of presidents being able to change the ideological balance of the Court are:

- George H. W. Bush (1991): replacing Thurgood Marshall (liberal) with Clarence Thomas (conservative)
- George W. Bush (2006): replacing Sandra O'Connor (moderate) with Samuel Alito (conservative)

Because these appointments are for life, the president's legacy remains on the Court well after the end of his presidency. Sandra O'Connor was appointed to the Court by Reagan in 1981 and remained on the Court for 25 years.

The president's support or criticism of the Court — Revised

The second power of the president relating to the Court is an *informal* one. The president can decide whether or not to throw his political weight and support behind decisions of the Court. This is more important when the president himself is popular, for then the president's support adds credibility to the Court while his opposition makes it appear less legitimate. Recent examples of presidents using this power are:

- George W. Bush's support for the Court's decision in *Zelman* v. *Simmons-Harris* (2002), upholding a school voucher programme in Ohio
- Barack Obama's criticism of the Court's decision in *Citizens United* v. *Federal Election Commission* (2010), striking down parts of the 2002 Bipartisan Campaign Reform Act.

Obama actually criticised the decision during his 2010 State of the Union Address with six of the Court's nine members seated in the front rows. Justice Alito was spotted mouthing the words 'not true' as the President delivered his criticism of the decision.

The Court's power over the president — Revised

The Supreme Court has one important power relating to the president in that it can declare the president's actions — and those of any member of the executive branch — unconstitutional. Consider the following three examples:

- *United States* v. *Richard M. Nixon* (1974): the Court declared that Nixon's refusal to hand over the 'White House tapes' — concerning the Watergate affair — was unconstitutional.
- *William Jefferson Clinton* v. *Paula Corbin Jones* (1997): the Court declared that Clinton had to face charges of sexual harassment made

by Ms Jones while he was still president rather than waiting until he left office. It was this case that led to President Clinton having to answer questions posed by Ms Jones's lawyers, including ones concerning a possible relationship between the President and a White House employee named Monica Lewinsky.

- *Rasul* v. *Bush* (2004): the Supreme Court ruled that the detainees at Guantánamo Bay did have access to the US federal courts to challenge their detention, thereby striking down an important part of the Bush administration's legal policy regarding the war on terror.

Thus the relations between the president and the Supreme Court are largely determined by the checks and balances that each has on the other.

Now test yourself

32 What is the president's one formal power relating to the Supreme Court?

33 Why were the appointments of Thomas (1991) and Alito (2006) to the Court so significant?

34 What is the president's one informal power relating to the Court?

35 Name two Court decisions that illustrate this power.

36 What is the Court's one power relating to the president?

37 Name two Court decisions that illustrate this power.

Tested

Factors that affect the presidency

Factors that can limit presidential power — Revised

There are two popular misconceptions about the US presidency. The first is that it is purely a one-man band. Although 'the president' might be thought of as such, 'the presidency' is much more like an orchestra, and a large one at that, made up of literally hundreds of people. The second misconception is that the president is hugely powerful — 'the most powerful person in the world' is a much-used phrase. Again, although there may be a grain of truth in this, students of US politics need to know that the office of the US president is often limited and, for its occupant, hugely frustrating. The presidency is therefore something of a paradox.

The more you realise the limits on presidential power, the better will be your understanding of the paradoxes of the office of the US presidency. What are these limits? We have already seen how Congress and the Supreme Court can limit the president. But there are five other factors with potential limits on the presidency.

1 *Public opinion*. President Clinton discovered how important public opinion was to being president. He survived his many scandals mainly because his public opinion ratings remained high. President Nixon saw the other side of that coin.

2 *Pressure groups*. Pressure groups can mobilise public opinion either for or against the president himself or his policies (see Chapter 3).

3 *The media*. All modern-day presidents live in an era where the media can profoundly limit what they can do — ask Obama or George W. Bush. The media's coverage of the president as a person is also critical.

4 *The federal bureaucracy*. The president is only one person in an executive branch made up of 15 executive departments and some 60 other federal government agencies, boards and commissions employing around 3 million civil servants. Getting the federal bureaucracy to do things can be a challenge to any president.

5 *Federalism.* It is not just the federal government that limits the president. Many federal government programmes have to be implemented by state and local governments across the entire USA.

Factors that can enhance presidential power

We have looked at the limits on the president's power. Let's now look at the other side of the coin: the factors that could enhance his ability to persuade, bargain and get things done — the factors that might help him to be a successful president.

> **Debate**
>
> Factors that limit and factors that enhance presidential power

1 *Size of the mandate at the last election.* In 2000, George W. Bush won only 48% of the popular vote and beat his opponent Al Gore 271–266 in the Electoral College. Contrast that with Ronald Reagan's win in 1984 when he won 59% of the vote, 525–13 in the Electoral College, and 49 of the 50 states. Reagan had a much stronger mandate to govern than did Bush.

2 *First, rather than second, term.* Presidents often find it easier to govern in their first term. Since the passage of the 22nd Amendment, second-term presidents quickly come to be seen as 'lame ducks' and lose much of their political clout.

3 *Previous Washington experience.* A president who has a good deal of previous Washington experience often finds it easier to get things done because he understands how things in Washington work and knows the people with whom he must do deals. Thus presidents such as Johnson and George H. W. Bush may have an advantage over those such as Carter and George W. Bush.

4 *Oratorical skills.* Although there is more to being president than making good speeches and appearing on television, being a good speaker — even a good 'performer' — can be a big advantage. It was these skills that gave presidents Reagan and Clinton a big advantage over, for example, Carter or either of the Bushes.

5 *Competent senior White House staff.* Being a good picker of people, especially for key White House positions such as Chief of Staff, can prove critical. Clinton chose poorly in his first term and suffered for it. Obama has proved to be a shrewder judge of people.

6 *Crises.* Curiously, a crisis can help a president, provided it is well handled. People tend to 'rally round the flag' — and the president — at times of crisis. The obvious example was the transformation of the George W. Bush presidency immediately after the attacks of 9/11. Equally, look at the way his presidency fell apart in 2005 after people's perception of government bungling in the aftermath of Hurricane Katrina.

An imperial presidency?

So on the one hand the presidency seems weak, limited and checked. But this is not how some scholars of the presidency have always regarded it. Some have written of an **imperial presidency**, a term popularised by the book of that title written in 1973 by Arthur Schlesinger.

According to Schlesinger, 'the imperial presidency was essentially the creation of foreign policy'. But there is a debate for and against Schlesinger's theory.

> **Imperial presidency** is a term used to refer to a presidency characterised by the misuse and abuse of power and high-handedness in dealing with Congress.

Those who support it point out that the presidency — especially during the administrations of Johnson (1963–69) and Nixon (1969–74) — has sometimes exhibited the following characteristics:

- increased use of war-making powers
- excessive secrecy
- high-handedness in dealing with Congress
- illegal activity
- the failure of the traditional checks and balances to work effectively

But others have argued against it, pointing out that the theory contains significant flaws. They point out that:

- Johnson was forced to decide not to stand for re-election in 1968
- Nixon was forced to resign in 1974
- as Ford — who followed Nixon — pointed out, 'Our Constitution works', including its checks and balances
- by the late 1970s there was much talk of an 'imperilled presidency' which was weak and ineffective

Be that as it may, Congress reacted to the imperial presidency claims by passing new laws to try to check the president's power, most notably the War Powers Act (1973) which was meant to limit the president's war-making power. But much of this legislation has proved to be somewhat ineffective.

Debate

For and against the imperial presidency thesis

Now test yourself

Tested ☐

38 Name the five factors, other than Congress and the Supreme Court, which potentially limit the power of the president.

39 Which six factors may enhance a president's ability to get things done?

40 Define the term 'the imperial presidency'.

41 Which author popularised the phrase in 1973?

42 Which five characteristics are associated with the imperial presidency?

43 Which two presidents are thought to have most clearly exhibited these characteristics?

44 What four flaws are there in the imperial presidency thesis?

45 Name a piece of legislation passed by Congress in 1973 to try to check the imperial presidency.

Answers on pp. 111–112

Exam practice

A Short answer questions:

  1 How much influence does the president have over legislation? [15]

  2 How does a president try to persuade members of Congress to support him? [15]

  3 What arguments were made for and against there being an 'imperial presidency'? [15]

B Essay questions:

  1 Is the president's power only 'the power to persuade'? [45]

  2 To what extent do presidents control foreign policy? [45]

  3 Assess the importance of the president's cabinet. [45]

Answers and quick quiz 7 online

Online ☐

8 The Supreme Court

The justices

Membership of the Court

There are a number of key points to remember regarding the membership of and the appointment process to the Supreme Court:

- There are nine members of the Supreme Court: one chief justice; eight associate justices (see Table 8.1).
- The number is fixed by Congress and has remained unchanged since 1869.
- They are appointed by the president.
- They are subject to confirmation by the Senate by a simple majority.
- They hold office for life 'during good behaviour' (Article III, Section 1 of the Constitution), meaning they can be impeached, tried and removed from office by Congress; otherwise justices leave the Court only by voluntary retirement or death.

Appointment process

The appointment process is conducted as follows:

1 The president must wait for a vacancy to occur: on average about once every 2 years, though Carter (1977–81) made no appointments and no vacancies occurred between 1994 and 2005.
2 The president's closest aides begin the search for suitable candidates.
3 A shortlist is drawn up and candidates are subjected to a detailed interview and FBI background checks.

Table 8.1 Supreme Court membership (2011)

Justice	Date appointed	Appointed by: president (party)
Chief Justice:		
John Roberts	2005	George W. Bush (R)
Associate Justices:		
Antonin Scalia	1986	Ronald Reagan (R)
Anthony Kennedy	1988	Ronald Reagan (R)
Clarence Thomas	1991	George H. W. Bush (R)
Ruth Bader Ginsburg	1993	Bill Clinton (D)
Stephen Breyer	1994	Bill Clinton (D)
Samuel Alito	2006	George W. Bush (R)
Sonia Sotomayor	2009	Barack Obama (D)
Elena Kagan	2010	Barack Obama (D)

4 The president announces the nominee at a public gathering at the White House.

5 The American Bar Association (ABA) traditionally offered a professional rating of the nominee (see Table 8.2).

6 The nominee (plus other witnesses) appears before a hearing at the Senate Judiciary Committee.

7 The Senate Judiciary Committee votes on whether or not to recommend confirmation.

8 The nomination is debated on the floor of the Senate.

9 A final vote is taken — a simple majority is required for confirmation.

Typical mistakes

The Senate Judiciary Committee's vote is only a recommendation, though it is rarely overturned. But don't say that the committee 'confirms' the nomination. Only the full Senate can do that.

Table 8.2 ABA ratings and Senate votes on selected Supreme Court nominees

Nominee	Year	ABA rating	Senate Judiciary Committee vote	Senate vote
Robert Bork	1987	Well qualified	5–9	42–58
Clarence Thomas	1991	Qualified	7–7	52–48
Ruth Bader Ginsburg	1993	Well qualified	18–0	96–3
Elena Kagan	2010	Well qualified	13–6	63–37

When the president is searching for a new member of the Supreme Court, where will he look? There are four main pools of recruitment:

- the federal Appeals Court (e.g. Sonia Sotomayor)
- the state courts (e.g. Sandra Day O'Connor, 1981–2006)
- the executive branch (e.g. Elena Kagan)
- academia (e.g. Elena Kagan)

Eight of the current members of the Court (2011) have previously served as judges of the federal appeal courts. Kagan had previously served as Solicitor General in the Justice Department and as Dean of Harvard Law School.

The Senate has rejected 12 Supreme Court nominees since 1789, the most recent being Robert Bork in 1987. Before that, President Nixon lost two nominees in as many years — Clement Haynsworth (45–55) in 1969 and Harrold Carswell (45–51) in 1970.

Typical mistakes

Harriet Miers (nominated to the Supreme Court by President George W. Bush in 2005) was not rejected. She withdrew from the process after criticism of her lack of experience. So she should not be given as an example of someone whom the Senate rejected.

Philosophy of justices

Revised

It is often suggested that presidents look for justices who share their judicial philosophy. In this respect, justices are classified as to whether they are 'liberals' or 'conservatives'. Another classification used is of **loose constructionists** and **strict constructionists** (see Table 8.3).

There are exceptions. President George H. W. Bush did not realise when he appointed David Souter to the Court in 1990 that he was appointing one of its most liberal members. Other justices — like Anthony Kennedy — are much less easy to classify. They tend to be referred to as **'swing' justices**.

A **loose constructionist** is a justice of the Supreme Court who interprets the Constitution in a loose or liberal fashion. A **strict constructionist** is a justice of the Supreme Court who interprets the Constitution in a strict, literal or conservative fashion.

Examiner's tip

These are technical, legal terms. Think of the word 'construction' as meaning 'interpretation'.

Table 8.3 Classification of Supreme Court justices

Classification	Ideology	Characteristics	Party	Examples
Strict constructionists	Conservative	Strict/literal interpretation of the Constitution; favour states' rights	Tend to be appointed by Republican presidents	Roberts Scalia Thomas Alito
Loose constructionists	Liberal	Read things into the Constitution; favour federal government power	Tend to be appointed by Democratic presidents	Ginsburg Breyer Sotomayor Kagan

1 How many justices make up the Supreme Court?
2 Who nominates them?
3 How are they confirmed?
4 How long a term do they serve?
5 What is the most common pool of recruitment for Supreme Court justices?
6 What is the difference between strict and loose constructionists?
7 Give an example of each from the current Court.
8 How would you classify Justice Anthony Kennedy?

The power of judicial review

Origins — Revised

Judicial review is nowhere mentioned in the Constitution. One might say that the Court 'found' the power for itself in the 1803 case of *Marbury v. Madison*. This was the first time that the Supreme Court declared an act of Congress unconstitutional.

> **Judicial review** is the power of the Supreme Court to declare acts of Congress, or actions of the executive — or acts or actions of state governments — unconstitutional, and thereby null and void.

Usage — Revised

Since then, the Supreme Court has used this power on hundreds of occasions — at times sparingly (periods of **judicial restraint**), but at other times far more frequently (periods of **judicial activism**). By using its power of judicial review, the Court can, in effect, update the meaning of the words of the Constitution, most of which were written over two centuries ago. Hence, they will decide what the phrase in the 8th Amendment (written in 1791) forbidding 'cruel and unusual punishments' means today. Likewise, they will decide whether the 1st Amendment right of 'freedom of speech' applies to the internet. As former Chief Justice Charles Evans Hughes once remarked: 'We are under a Constitution, but the Constitution is what the judges say it is.'

> **Judicial activism** is an approach to judicial decision making which holds that a judge should use his or her position to promote desirable social ends.
>
> **Judicial restraint** is an approach to judicial decision making which holds that a judge should defer to the legislative and executive branches and should put great stress on the precedent established in previous Court decisions.

Strict constructionists tend to favour judicial restraint; loose constructionists tend to favour judicial activism — but note the word 'tend'.

Constitutional basis Revised

When the Constitution was written, there was a good deal of concern that the new federal government had been given too much power over the states and individuals. It was partly to allay those fears that the first 10 amendments — known as the Bill of Rights — were added. But it was not until the passage of the 14th Amendment in 1868 that the Constitution explicitly began to restrict the action that *states* could take against individual citizens. This was done through two provisions of this Amendment — the equal protection clause and the due process clause. The Court's use of the due process provision of the 14th Amendment — preventing states from depriving persons of 'life, liberty, or property without **due process** of law' — has enabled the Court to review and strike down a wide range of state legislation.

> **Due process** (of law) can mean either (1) substantive due process: the requirement that the substance of the law be administered fairly, reasonably and constitutionally; or (2) procedural due process: the requirement that the process of the law must be fair.

Now test yourself Tested

9 What is the power of judicial review?
10 How did it come about?
11 What is meant by (a) judicial activism and (b) judicial restraint?
12 How did the Constitution provide for restricting the action of the states against individual citizens?
13 What is meant by (a) substantive due process and (b) procedural due process?

Political significance of the Court

The political significance of the Court is that it makes decisions in politically important and controversial matters of public policy, such as freedom of speech, gun control, abortion rights and affirmative action programmes. These are policy issues concerning which politicians from the major parties often fundamentally disagree and which feature quite prominently in many election campaigns, presidential as well as congressional. Any institution that makes decisions about these kinds of political controversies is of great political significance.

Using its power of judicial review, the Supreme Court has involved itself in a host of political issues. It also does this through its role as a guarantor of fundamental **civil rights** and **liberties**.

The Supreme Court can also be seen as something of a 'political body' because its members are appointed by a politician (the president) and confirmed by other politicians (senators). Appointments to the Supreme Court also become an issue in many presidential elections. This was certainly the case in the 2000 election.

One can see clearly — some might say too clearly — the political significance of the Supreme Court in the case of *George W. Bush* v. *Albert*

> **Civil rights** are positive acts of government designed to protect persons against arbitrary or discriminatory treatment by government or individuals.
> **Civil liberties** are those liberties that guarantee the protection of persons, expression and property from arbitrary interference by the government.

> **Typical mistakes**
> A common focus for essay questions is the Court's political significance. Don't forget to deal with the appointment process and the power of judicial review — both are important here.

Gore Jr (2000). Five weeks after the presidential election, on 11 December 2000, the Supreme Court ruled that the manual recount scheme devised by the Florida Supreme Court was unconstitutional because it violated the 'equal protection' clause of the 14th Amendment. In the same decision, the Court also ruled that given the time constraints, 'it is evident that any recount seeking to meet the December 12 [deadline] will be unconstitutional'. The Court was seen by some to be literally handing the election to Governor Bush.

Freedom of religion ───────────────────────────── Revised ☐

- *Allegheny County* v. *American Civil Liberties Union* (1989): the Court declared Allegheny (Pennsylvania) County's Christmas display an infringement of 1st Amendment rights because it contained only religious figures, whereas in 1984 (*Lynch* v. *Donnelly*) the Court had okayed the City of Pawtucket's (Rhode Island) display, which included religious figures but also Santa Claus and a Christmas tree.
- *Lee* v. *Weisman* (1992): the Court declared prayer at public (i.e. state) school graduation ceremonies unconstitutional.
- *Zelman* v. *Simmons–Harris* (2002): the Court upheld Ohio's so-called 'school voucher' programme as being neutral in terms of religion.
- *McCreary County* v. *American Civil Liberties Union of Kentucky* (2005) and *Van Orden* v. *Perry* (2005): the Court ruled on the display of the Ten Commandments in public places, finding the Kentucky commandments unconstitutional but the Texas ones (*Van Orden*) constitutional.

> **Examiner's tip**
>
> When using these cases in an answer, don't get side-tracked by the narrative. What happened to whom is really not important. Concentrate on the analytical importance of the case.

> **Typical mistakes**
>
> Don't misunderstand the term 'public school' as used in the USA. It refers to state-run schools, not private schools as in the UK.

Freedom of speech and expression ───────────────── Revised ☐

- *Texas* v. *Johnson* (1989): a Texas state law forbidding the burning of the US flag was declared unconstitutional by the Court. (President George H. W. Bush described the Court's decision as 'wrong, dead wrong'.)
- *Watchtower Bible and Tract Society* v. *Village of Stratton, Ohio* (2002): the Court struck down a law which required people going door-to-door (e.g. politicians, sales persons) to get a permit beforehand.
- *Citizens United* v. *Federal Election Commission* (2010): the Court ruled that in terms of rights of political speech (and therefore making financial donations to political campaigns), business corporations have the same rights as individuals, thereby overturning key provisions of the 2002 Bipartisan Campaign Reform Act.
- *Snyder* v. *Phelps* (2011): the Court upheld the right of a fringe church group to stage anti-gay protests at military funerals.

Right to bear arms ───────────────────────────── Revised ☐

- *United States* v. *Lopez* (1995): the Court declared unconstitutional the 1990 Gun-Free School Zones Act, stating that Congress had exceeded its power under Article I, Section 8 of the Constitution. This case was one that also had clear implications for the scope of federal government power over state and local jurisdictions.

- *Printz* v. *United States* (1997): the Court declared unconstitutional part of the 1993 Brady Act requiring local law enforcement officers to conduct background checks on would-be handgun purchasers during a 5-day waiting period. Here was another ruling clearly affecting the federal–state government balance.
- *District of Columbia* v. *Heller* (2008): the Court declared unconstitutional a law passed by the District of Columbia in 1976 banning the ownership of handguns and requiring shotguns and rifles to be kept unloaded and either disassembled or trigger-locked. The Court stated for the first time that, in its interpretation, the 2nd Amendment right to 'keep and bear arms' is an individual, rather than merely a collective, right.

Rights of arrested persons

Revised

- *Gideon* v. *Wainwright* (1963): the Court interpreted the 14th Amendment as guaranteeing the right to legal representation.
- *Miranda* v. *Arizona* (1966): the Court interpreted the 5th Amendment right to remain silent as extending to the right to be reminded of that right when arrested.
- *Berghuis* v. *Thompkins* (2010): the Court ruled that suspects having been reminded of their right to remain silent must say that they want to remain silent, otherwise questioning may continue.

Capital punishment

Revised

- *Furman* v. *Georgia* (1972): the Court decided that the death penalty, as then imposed, was a 'cruel and unusual punishment' and thereby violated the 8th Amendment. The consequences of this case included the more widespread use of lethal injection and of two-stage trials, in which, during a second stage, mitigating circumstances are considered before the sentence is decided.

> **Typical mistakes**
> It is important to include the phrase 'as then imposed'. The case did not declare capital punishment itself to be unconstitutional.

- *Atkins* v. *Virginia* (2002): the Court ruled that the execution of mentally retarded criminals was unconstitutional.
- *Roper* v. *Simmons* (2005): the Court ruled that it was unconstitutional to sentence anyone to death for a crime they committed when younger than 18.
- *Baze* v. *Rees* (2008): the Court decided that lethal injection — the method used by the federal government and 35 states to execute criminals — did not violate the 8th Amendment ban on 'cruel and unusual punishment'.

Rights of racial minorities

Revised

- *Brown* v. *Board of Education of Topeka* (1954): the Court declared a law of the state of Kansas to be unconstitutional because it transgressed the 'equal protection' clause of the 14th Amendment. It led to the desegregation of schools across the USA, especially in the Deep South.

'Separate educational facilities are inherently unequal', declared the Court, overturning its 1896 ruling of 'separate but equal'.

- *Swann* v. *Charlotte–Mecklenberg Board of Education* (1971): the Court extended the ban on segregated schools from *de jure* segregation (mainly in the South) to *de facto* segregation (mainly in the cities of the Northeast) caused by the widespread policy of neighbourhood schooling. It led to the introduction of school busing programmes to provide racially mixed schools in all areas.

- *Adarand Constructors* v. *Peña* (1995): the Court struck down a federal government affirmative action programme on the employment of minority workers. This case led to President Clinton's remark about affirmative action: 'Mend it, don't end it.'

- *Gratz* v. *Bollinger* (2003): the Court ruled that the University of Michigan's affirmative action-based undergraduate admissions programme was unconstitutional because it was too 'mechanistic'.

- *Parents Involved in Community Schools Inc.* v. *Seattle School District No. 1* (2007) and *Meredith* v. *Jefferson County (Kentucky) Board of Education* (2007): the Court declared it unconstitutional to assign students to public (i.e. state) schools solely for the purpose of achieving racial balance.

> **Typical mistakes**
>
> Some students mention only the *Brown* v. *Board of Education of Topeka* case in their essays, failing to realise that a case from nearly 60 years ago does not fulfil the need to be up-to-date. Mention this case briefly, but then also mention more recent cases, especially *Gratz* v. *Bollinger*.

Abortion rights

Revised ☐

- *Roe* v. *Wade* (1973): the Court struck down a Texas state law forbidding abortion. It interpreted the 14th Amendment right of 'liberty' to include 'freedom of personal choice in matters of marriage and family life', and held that this right 'necessarily includes the right of a woman to decide whether or not to terminate her pregnancy'. Few cases have been of such profound political importance. The phrase 'personal choice' gives rise to those who support abortion rights calling themselves 'pro-choice'.

> **Typical mistakes**
>
> Again, as above, don't fall into the trap of using only this 1973 case. Try to ensure you also mention *Gonzales* v. *Carhart*.

- *Webster* v. *Reproductive Health Services* (1989): the Court upheld a state law of Missouri forbidding the involvement of any 'public employee' or 'public facility' in the performance of an abortion 'not necessary to save the life of the mother'. 'Pro-choice' supporters regarded this as the Court nibbling away at *Roe* v. *Wade*.

- *Planned Parenthood of Southeastern Pennsylvania* v. *Casey* (1992): the Court upheld a Pennsylvania state law that required a married woman seeking an abortion to receive counselling on the risks and alternatives and to wait 24 hours after receiving counselling. Women under 18 also had to have parental consent for an abortion. This again was opposed by the 'pro-choice' lobby. But the 'pro-life' supporters were also angry, as they wanted the Court to go all the way and overturn *Roe* v. *Wade*. However, the Court struck down the provision in the Pennsylvania state law which required a married woman to notify her spouse before undergoing an abortion.

- *Gonzales* v. *Carhart* (2007): the Court upheld the Partial-Birth Abortion Ban Act passed by Congress in 2003. This was the first time the Court had declared that a specific abortion procedure could be banned and made no exception for the health of the woman, although it did provide an exception if the life of the mother was threatened.

Tested

Now test yourself

14 Define (a) civil rights and (b) civil liberties.
15 What two factors contribute towards the Supreme Court being seen as a 'political body'?
16 What was significant about the decision in *Citizens United* v. *FEC* (2010)?
17 What did the Court decide about citizens' 2nd Amendment rights in *District of Columbia* v. *Heller* (2008)?
18 How did the Court protect the rights of arrested persons in the *Gideon* and *Miranda* decisions?
19 How has the Court limited the use of the death penalty since 2002?
20 Give two examples of recent Court decisions regarding the rights of racial minorities.
21 What was important about the decision in *Gonzales* v. *Carhart* (2007)?

Checks on the Court

Just like the Congress and the presidency, the Supreme Court is also subject to checks and balances — some formal (i.e. they are mentioned in the Constitution) and some informal.

> **Examiner's tip**
>
> These checks would form a significant part of an answer to a question about whether or not the Supreme Court has 'too much power'. Clearly the Court does have a good deal of power, but it is also subject to significant checks.

Checks by Congress
Revised

- The Senate confirms all Supreme Court appointments.
- The House can impeach justices and the Senate try them and, if found guilty by a two-thirds majority, they can be removed from office.
- Congress can alter the number of justices on the Court.
- Congress can initiate constitutional amendments, thereby seeking to overturn judgments of the Court with which it disagrees, such as recent (though unsuccessful) attempts concerning flag desecration, school prayers, abortion rights and congressional term limits.

> **Examiner's tip**
>
> This also relates to the issue of the Court and accountability. The Court can be thought of as accountable through the confirmation process in the Senate (although that is before the justices take office) and also through the threat of impeachment.

Checks by the president
Revised

- The president nominates all justices.
- He can decide either to throw his political weight behind the Court (e.g. George W. Bush over *Zelman* v. *Simmons-Harris* in 2002) or to criticise it openly (e.g. George H. W. Bush over flag-burning in 1990, and Barack Obama over *Citizens United* v. *FEC* in 2010).
- He has the power of pardon (see p. 85).

Other checks
Revised

- The Court has no enforcement powers (e.g. in the *Brown* v. *Board of Education of Topeka* decision it was dependent upon President Eisenhower sending in federal troops to desegregate the Little Rock Central High School in 1957).
- The Court has no initiation power. It has to wait for cases to come before it. It cannot rule on hypothetical issues.

- Public opinion can be a check on the Court (e.g. the *Planned Parenthood of Southeastern Pennsylvania* v. *Casey* decision on abortion rights in 1992).
- Some parts of the Constitution are unambiguous and therefore not open to interpretation by the Court.
- The Supreme Court may check itself by reversing earlier decisions. Having ruled in 1989 (*Stanford* v. *Kentucky*) that states could execute 16- and 17-year-old offenders, the Court ruled in 2003 (*Roper* v. *Simmons*) that such executions were unconstitutional. In 2000 (*Stenberg* v. *Carhart*), the Court declared a Nebraska state law prohibiting late-term abortions to be unconstitutional, but in 2007 (*Gonzales* v. *Carhart*) it upheld an almost identical federal law.

Now test yourself

22 What four checks does Congress have on the Supreme Court?

23 Give an example of a president (a) supporting and (b) criticising a Supreme Court decision.

24 Give an example of the Court checking itself by reversing an earlier decision.

Answers on p. 112

Tested

Exam practice

A Short answer questions:

    1 How do Republican-appointed justices tend to differ from Democrat-appointed justices?   [15]

    2 Using examples, explain the checks on the Supreme Court's powers.   [15]

    3 Why are appointments to the Supreme Court so controversial?   [15]

B Essay questions:

    1 Why can the Supreme Court be regarded as a political institution?   [45]

    2 How successful has the Supreme Court been at protecting individual rights and liberties?   [45]

    3 Is the Supreme Court too powerful for an unelected body?   [45]

Answers and quick quiz 8 online

Online

Now test yourself answers

Chapter 1 Elections and voting

1 Every 4 years.

2 A natural-born US citizen; at least 35 years of age; resident of the USA for at least 14 years.

3 May serve a maximum of only two terms.

4 Primary is an election; caucus is a meeting.

5 Show popularity of presidential candidates; choose delegates to go to the National Party Convention.

6 Open primary: any registered voter may vote in either primary; closed primary: only registered Republicans may vote in the Republican primary, and only registered Democrats may vote in the Democratic primary.

7 Proportional primary: delegates are awarded to candidates in proportion to the votes they win; winner-takes-all primary: winner of the popular vote gets all the delegates.

8 The phenomenon by which states schedule their presidential primary or caucus earlier in the cycle in an attempt to increase their importance in the choosing of candidates.

9 The year or so before the start of the primaries when potential candidates try to gain name recognition and money as well as put together the necessary organisation.

10 See p. 11.

11 Choosing/confirming the presidential candidate; choosing/confirming the vice-presidential candidate; deciding on the party platform.

12 When the presidential candidate chooses a vice-presidential candidate who is different in terms of region, political experience, age, gender, etc.

13 The statement of a party's policies for an upcoming presidential election.

14 Promoting party unity; enthusing the party faithful; enthusing ordinary voters.

15 Any three of: first opportunity to address ordinary voters; chance to display presidential qualities to voters; chance to outline policies; boost opinion ratings.

16 Labor Day (first Monday of September).

17 Intra-party: within one party; inter-party: between the two parties.

18 8–9 weeks.

19 On television.

20 John McCain and Russell Feingold.

21 National Party Committees banned from raising or spending 'soft money'; labour unions and corporate groups forbidden from directly funding issue advertisements; the banning of union or corporate money to fund advertisements that mention a federal candidate, within 60 days of a general election or 30 days of a primary; the prohibition of fundraising on federal property; increased individual limits on contributions to individual candidates or candidate committees to $2,300

(2007–08), to be increased for inflation in each odd-numbered year; banned contributions from foreign nationals; 'Stand By Your Ad' provision, resulting in all campaign ads including a verbal endorsement by the candidate with the words: 'I'm [candidate's name] and I approve this message'.

22 1960

23 1992

24 Incumbents have a record to defend and can have their words from 4 years ago quoted back at them.

25 Reinforcement and activation.

26 According to each state's representation in Congress.

27 270

28 Winner-takes-all.

29 (a) Preserves the voice of the small-population states; promotes a two-horse race; (b) Small-population states over-represented; winner-takes-all system can distort the result; possible for winner of popular vote to lose in Electoral College; unfair to national third parties; 'rogue' or 'faithless' Electors; the system used in the case of an Electoral College deadlock could result in the House choosing a president of one party and the Senate choosing a vice-president of another party.

30 Likely to lead to a multi-candidate election with the winner gaining maybe only 35-40% of the votes.

31 The party which has the highest level of support from its own identifiers usually wins.

32 Abortion, defence, law and order, gun control, women's rights.

33 Democrats have strongly supported civil rights for African-Americans.

34 Protestants tend to vote Republican; Catholics tend to vote Democrat.

35 Democrat vote has declined; Republican vote has increased.

36 The Midwest.

37 The economy.

38 Typical Democrat voting blocs: blue-collar, unionised workers; urban dwellers; West and Northeast; Catholic; Jewish; racial minority, possibly black or Hispanic; female; liberal; less wealthy; less well educated. Typical Republican voting blocs: white-collar, professional workers; suburban and rural; sun-belt; Protestant, especially evangelical; white; male; conservative; wealthy; college-educated.

39 Whole of the House of Representatives; one-third of the Senate.

40 Elections that occur midway through the president's 4-year term of office.

41 House: at least 25 years old and US citizen for at least 7 years; Senate: at least 30 years old and US citizen for at least 9 years.

42 A geographic division of a state from which a member of the House of Representatives is elected.

43 A state law that requires House members to be resident within the congressional district they represent.

44 The effect of a strong candidate for a party at the top of the ticket (i.e. president, state governor) helping congressional candidates of the same party to get elected at the same time.

45 The practice of voting for candidates of two or more parties for different offices at the same election.

46 House: mostly over 90%; Senate: between 79% and 96%.

47 Loses seats in both houses of Congress.

48 A mechanism by which citizens of a state can place proposed laws, and in some states constitutional amendments, on the state ballot.

49 24

50 Direct: proposals that qualify to go directly on the ballot; indirect: proposals that are submitted to the state legislature, which decides on further action.

51 Ban on same-sex marriage; increase in state minimum wage.

52 (a) Advantages: provide a way of enacting reforms on controversial issues that state legislatures are often unwilling or unable to act upon; increase the responsiveness and accountability of state legislatures; can help increase voter turnout; increase citizen interest in state issues and may also encourage pressure group membership; (b) Disadvantages: lack the flexibility of the legislative process; vulnerable to manipulation by special interests.

53 An electoral device, available in all 50 states, by which voters can effectively veto a bill passed by the state legislature.

54 A procedure that enables voters in a state to remove an elected official from office before their term has expired.

Chapter 2 Political parties

1 Federalism.

2 National committee; party chairman; national convention.

3 Process for candidate selection.

4 The economy, civil rights, role of the federal government.

5 Liberal: a view that seeks to change the political, economic and social status quo in favour of the well-being, rights and liberties of the individual, and especially those who are generally disadvantaged.

6 Conservative: a view that seeks to defend the political, economic and social status quo and therefore tends to oppose changes in the institutions and structures of society.

7 Democrats — liberal; Republicans — conservative.

8 The South used to vote solidly for the Democratic Party.

9 Has dramatically collapsed.

10 (a) Red America: states that tend to vote Republican; (b) blue America: states that tend to vote Democrat.

11 (a) Red America: male; white; Protestant; wealthy; rural; Southern or Midwestern; conservative; (b) blue America: female; rainbow coalition; Catholic; less wealthy; urban; Northeast, Great Lakes and west coast; liberal.

12 Any two of: the shift of southern conservative Democrats to the Republican Party; the end of the Cold War consensus in foreign policy following the demise of the Soviet Union; the polarising presidencies of Bill Clinton, George W. Bush and Barack Obama; the effect of the 'new media' such as direct mail, talk radio, cable television and the internet.

13 A party system in which two major parties regularly win the vast majority of votes in general elections, regularly capture nearly all of the seats in the legislature, and alternately control the executive branch of government.

14 First-past-the-post, winner-takes-all electoral system; all-embracing nature of the two major parties.

15 Fifty-party system; one-party system; no-party system.

16 The theory, popular in the last three decades of the twentieth century, that political parties were in decline in terms of membership, functions and importance.

17 The theory that suggests that parties, far from being in decline, are increasingly important in elections, fundraising and organisation, and in Congress.

18 Two.

19 One.

20 Electoral system; federal campaign finance laws; state ballot access laws; lack of resources; lack of media coverage; lack of well-known, well-qualified candidates; regarded as too ideological; the tactics of the two major parties.

Chapter 3 Pressure groups

1 An organised interest group in which members hold similar beliefs and actively pursue ways to influence government.

2 Pressure groups seek to influence those who control government whereas political parties seek to win control of government.

3 See Table 3.1.

4 Representation, citizen participation, public education, agenda building and programme monitoring.

5 Attempt to influence the agendas of political parties, legislators and bureaucracies to give prominence and priority to their interests.

6 Fundraising; endorsing and opposing candidates; publishing voter guides.

7 An attempt to exert influence on the policy-making, legislative or judicial process by individuals or organised groups.

8 Television ads; journal advertising; roadside hoardings; bumper stickers; badges.

9 Postal blitzes on members of Congress, the White House or a government department, marches and demonstrations.

10 The more diverse a society is, the greater will be the variety of special interests to represent.

11 Congressional committees; state government.

12 Parties are therefore not seen as the only groups which organise political activity.

13 Direct contact with House and Senate members and their senior staff; direct contact with the relevant House and Senate committee members and their staff; organising constituents to write to, phone, fax, e-mail or visit their House and Senate members to express their support for or opposition to a certain policy initiative; publicising the voting records of House and Senate members; endorsement of supportive members and opposition to non-supportive members in forthcoming re-election campaigns; fundraising, campaigning for or against members of Congress — paying for radio/television advertisements etc.

14 A pressure group supporting female congressional candidates, helping them to raise money early in the electoral cycle.

15 A 'friend of the Court' brief in which a pressure group presents its views to the Court before oral arguments are heard.

16 *McCreary County* v. *American Civil Liberties Union* (2005).

17 That America has 'the finest Congress that money can buy'.

18 Allows former members of Congress or the executive branch to take up highly paid jobs as lobbyists.

Chapter 4 Racial and ethnic politics

1 Emancipation of the slaves; immigration.

2 Four of: Irish Catholics; European Jews; Hispanics; refugees from Africa, the Middle East and Asia.

3 Showed Hispanics as a larger proportion of the US population than African-Americans.

4 Two of: New Mexico, Texas, California, Hawaii.

5 Positive acts of government designed to protect persons against arbitrary or discriminatory treatment by government or individuals.

6 Three of: bus boycotts and freedom riders in the South; March for Jobs and Freedom including Martin Luther King's 'I Have a Dream' speech; assassination of Martin Luther King; Million Man March.

7 Three of: Martin Luther King, Malcolm X, Louis Farrakhan, Jesse Jackson.

8 A programme that entails giving the members of a previously disadvantaged minority group a head start in such areas as higher education and employment.

9 Programmes perceived by some as being unfair to those of the majority (white) group.

10 A set-aside programme to benefit previously disadvantaged minorities in such areas as higher education and employment, by which a certain percentage (i.e. quota) of places is reserved for people of the previously disadvantaged group.

11 The existence within a nation state of people from many different cultures whose own learned patterns of behaviour lead to a diversity of culture in such matters as lifestyle, belief, custom and language.

12 African-Americans up from 21 (1984) to 42 (2011); Hispanics up from 10 (1984) to 26 (2011).

13 Increased for Republicans in 2004, but fell back to 2–1 advantage for Democrats in 2008.

14 Any four of: Eric Holder (African-American); Ken Salazar and Hilda Solis (Hispanics); Steven Chu and Gary Locke (Chinese-American); Eric Shinseki (Japanese-American); Ray LaHood (Lebanese-American).

15 Reagan: less than 5% of appointees were from racial minorities; Obama: 27.5% African-American and 7.1% Hispanic.

Chapter 5 The Constitution

1 A unitary form of government is one in which political power rests with one central/national government. A confederal form of government is one in which virtually all political power rests with the individual states, and very little with the central/ national government. A federal form of government is one in which some political power rests with the national (or federal) government but other, equally important, powers rest with the state governments.

2 Allocation of national government and state government powers; representation of the states in Congress; method of choosing the president.

3 A constitution that consists of a full and authoritative set of rules written down in a single text.

4 The 'general welfare clause'; the 'necessary and proper clause'.

5 Two of: presidential primaries; congressional committees; the president's cabinet; the Executive Office of the President; the Supreme Court's power of judicial review.

6 A theory of government whereby political power is distributed among three branches of government — the legislature, the executive and the judiciary — acting both independently and interdependently.

7 A principle that the size and scope of the federal government should be limited to that which is necessary for the common good of the people.

8 A system of government in which each branch — legislative, executive and judicial — exercises control over the actions of the other branches of government.

9 Powers.

10 The principle by which government and political power are vested not only in the federal government, but also in the state governments.

11 Literally, the rights, powers and duties of the state governments, but often used to denote opposition to increasing the federal government's power at the expense of that of the states.

12 A theory of government by which political power is divided between a national government and state governments, each having their own areas of substantive jurisdiction.

13 More decentralised.

14 Three of: the war in Iraq; homeland security issues following the attacks on the USA on 9/11 (2001); the expansion of the Medicare programme; the No Child Left Behind Act passed by Congress (2001); the Wall Street and banking collapse (2008).

15 Three of: not vetoing expensive federal government programmes; initially feeble response to Hurricane Katrina; taking control of Fannie Mae and Freddie Mac; Wall Street bailout package.

16 It was over.

17 Two of: the re-authorisation of the State Children's Health Insurance Program (SCHIP); the expansion of Medicaid under Obama's healthcare reform legislation; higher education expenditure (e.g. Pell Grants, 2010); $4.35 billion invested in the Race to the Top program to boost education in the states.

18 Healthcare reform.

19 Article I: the legislature, including the powers of Congress (Section 8); Article II: the executive, including the powers of the president (Section 2); Article III: the judiciary.

20 The Bill of Rights.

21 Two of: 14th: guarantees of 'equal protection' and 'due process' applied to all states; 16th: Congress given power to tax income; 17th: direct election of senators; 22nd: two-term limit for president; 25th: presidential disability and succession.

22 Either by Congress with a two-thirds majority in favour in both houses, or by a national Constitutional Convention called at the request of two-thirds of the state legislatures. The latter has never been used.

23 Either by three-quarters of the state legislatures or by three-quarters of the states holding a Constitutional Convention. The latter has been used only once — to ratify the 21st Amendment in 1933.

24 Two of: to require the federal government to pass a balanced budget; to impose term limits on members of Congress; to forbid desecration of the American flag.

25 (i) The Founding Fathers created a deliberately difficult amendment process; (ii) the vagueness of the Constitution, which has allowed the document to evolve without the need for constant formal amendment; (iii) the Supreme Court's power of judicial review; (iv) the reverence with which the Constitution is regarded, which makes many politicians cautious of tampering with it; (v) the experience of the 18th Amendment, regarding the prohibition of alcohol, which was repealed (by the 21st Amendment) just 14 years later.

26 The fundamental rights guaranteed by the federal Constitution, principally in the Bill of Rights — the first 10 amendments — but also in subsequent amendments.

27 Can pass laws to facilitate these rights as well as, through its committee system and investigative powers, call the executive branch to account regarding the way it implements the laws which Congress has passed.

28 Needs to implement the laws and programmes which Congress passes and establishes in order to ensure that legislation is followed by delivery.

29 One of: *Dred Scott* v. *Sandford* (1857); *Plessy* v. *Ferguson* (1896).

30 One of: abortion rights for women (*Roe* v. *Wade*); rights of arrested persons (*Gideon* v. *Wainwright* and *Miranda* v. *Arizona*); rights of racial minorities (*Brown* v. *Board of Education of Topeka*); gun rights (*District of Columbia* v. *Heller*).

31 One of: *Gratz* v. *Bollinger* (2003); *Gonzales* v. *Carhart* (2007).

Chapter 6 Congress

1 Two.

2 House: 435; Senate: 100.

3 House: proportional to population; Senate: two per state.

4 Women: House 72, Senate 17; African-Americans: House 42, Senate 0.

5 Increased.

6 Begin consideration of money bills; impeachment; elect president if Electoral College deadlocked.

7 To make a formal accusation, or to bring charges against someone.

8 Ratify treaties; confirm appointments; try cases of impeachment; elect vice-president if Electoral College deadlocked.

9 (a) two-thirds; (b) two-thirds.

10 Pass legislation; conduct investigations; initiate constitutional amendments; declare war; confirm a newly appointed vice-president.

11 Two-thirds in both houses.

12 Five; 1941.

13 (a) 50; (b) 0.

14 (a) Vice-president; (b) Speaker.

15 Three of: House Speaker; Majority and Minority Leaders of both houses; standing committee chairmen.

16 Acts as the presiding officer of the House; interprets and enforces the rules of the House, and decides points of order; refers bills to committees; appoints select and conference committee chairs; appoints majority party members of the House Rules Committee; may exercise considerable influence in the flow of legislation through the House, as well as in committee assignments for majority party members and even the selection of House standing committee chairs.

17 Standing committees; House Rules Committee; conference committees.

18 Senate: around 18; House: between 45 and 50.

19 In the same proportion as that which exists within the chamber as a whole.

20 That the chairman of a standing committee will be the member of the majority party with the longest continuous service on that committee.

21 To conduct the committee stage of the legislative process; to conduct investigations within the committee's policy area; (Senate only) to begin the confirmation process of numerous presidential appointments to both the executive and judicial branches of the federal government.

22 In the committee rooms.

23 Because the executive is physically separated from the legislature.

24 Timetables and prioritises bills for consideration on the floor of the House.

25 To reconcile the differences between the two versions (House version and Senate version) of the same bill.

26 The committee stage is as far as most bills get; committees have full power of amendment; committees have life-and-death power over bills.

27 A delaying tactic based on the right of senators to unlimited debate. Its main purpose is to delay or defeat a bill or nomination.

28 Sign the bill; leave the bill on his desk; veto the bill.

29 The power vested in the president by which he can return a bill to Congress unsigned.

30 Pass the bill again with a two-thirds majority in both houses.

31 US parties are far less centralised and ideologically cohesive than their UK counterparts; they do not have the 'sticks' and 'carrots' that their UK counterparts have as incentives to party unity; constituents control the selection of candidates — through congressional primaries; House members are subject to elections every 2 years, increasing their reliance on the views of their constituents; the executive branch does not depend for its existence

on getting its policies through the legislature, as it does in the UK.

32 One in which the majority of one party votes 'yes' while the majority of the other party votes 'no'.

33 The Constitution states that House and Senate members must be residents of the state they represent, so this gives them a good understanding of what 'the folks back home' are saying; some states go further by insisting that House members reside in the actual district (constituency) they represent; many House and Senate members will have been born and educated, lived and worked in the state/district they now represent; House members are especially careful about constituents' views as they have to face election every 2 years.

34 (i) How legislators represent the views of their constituents; (ii) how representative legislators are of society as a whole in such matters as race and gender.

35 Initiating legislation; making contact with members of Congress through phone calls and visits; making contact with senior members of the congressional staff, including committee staff.

36 Four of: contacts with members of Congress through phone calls and visits; contacts with senior members of the congressional staff; attempts to generate public support favourable to their position; provide evidence to relevant committee hearings to support their position; organise rallies and demonstrations — both in Washington DC and around the country; organise petition drives, e-mail campaigns, etc.; money raising to fund politicians who support their cause and to seek to defeat those who do not.

37 In January 2011, 20% approved and 73% disapproved of the job Congress was doing.

38 The failure to get action on policy proposals and legislation in Congress.

39 A complicated and lengthy legislative process in which those who want to pass bills must win at every stage; divided government; divided Congress; the filibuster in the Senate; the need for super-majorities (i.e. two-thirds, three-fifths) in certain instances; the lack of strict party discipline; 2-year terms of office for the House give a very short time frame for getting things done.

40 The Founding Fathers designed a system to provide limited government.

Chapter 7 The presidency

1 State of the Union Address.

2 Pass the bill again with a two-thirds majority in both houses.

3 Won 93% of them.

4 Article II.

5 Senate must confirm by a simple majority.

6 Congress's power of the purse, power to declare war and power to conduct investigations.

7 Ratified: START Treaty (2010); rejected: Comprehensive Test Ban Treaty (1999).

8 Former president Richard Nixon.

9 The advisory group selected by the president to aid him in making decisions and coordinating the work of the federal government.

10 Because they cannot be both in the cabinet and in Congress.

11 State governors, city mayors, academics, policy specialists.

12 Engender team spirit; look collegial and consultative; give information to all cabinet members; glean information from cabinet members — find out what is going on in each department; debate policies; present 'big picture' items such as the budget; check up on legislation going through Congress; see cabinet members he would not otherwise see.

13 Get-to-know-you sessions; sort out inter-departmental disputes; catching up with other members (before and/or after the meetings); an opportunity to see the president — whom many of them would not otherwise see; to gain them prestige back at their department, with first-hand news of what the president wants.

14 They have huge departments to run; they are not based in the White House; they have loyalties other than to the president.

15 They serve only the president; they have close proximity and access to the president.

16 The top staff agencies in the White House that give the president help and advice.

17 1939

18 The huge increase in the size and scale of the federal government.

19 White House Office, National Security Council, Office of Management and Budget.

20 Honest broker; passion for anonymity.

21 To help the president coordinate foreign and defence policy.

22 State Department, Defense Department, CIA, relevant congressional committees, Joint Chiefs of Staff.

23 To advise the president on the allocation of federal funds in the annual budget; to oversee the spending of all federal government departments and agencies.

24 'Separated institutions, sharing powers'.

25 (a) Amend/block; (b) override; (c) Senate confirmation; (d) Senate confirmation; (e) Senate ratification.

26 (a) Power to declare war, power of the purse; (b) powers of investigation, impeachment, trial, removal from office.

27 Persuade.

28 Vice-president, Office of Legislative Affairs, cabinet officers, party leaders in Congress.

29 Four of: make phone calls to selected members of Congress; offer help with legislation that benefits members' constituents; offer help with federal executive/judicial appointments of interest to constituents; invite members to a meeting at the White House; go to Capitol Hill to address a selected group of members; offer to campaign for members of his own party.

30 Bargainer-in-chief.

31 The annual statistic which measures how often the president won in roll-call votes in the House and Senate in which he took a clear position, expressed as a percentage of the whole.

32 Nominate justices.

33 They changed the ideological balance of the Court.

20366

Now test yourself answers

34 Decide whether or not to throw his political weight and support behind decisions of the Court.

35 *Zelman* v. *Simmons-Harris* (2002); *Citizens United* v. *Federal Election Commission* (2010).

36 Declare the president's actions unconstitutional.

37 Two of: *United States* v. *Richard Nixon* (1974); *William Jefferson Clinton* v. *Paula Corbin Jones* (1997); *Rasul* v. *Bush* (2004).

38 Public opinion; pressure groups; the media; the federal bureaucracy; federalism.

39 Size of the mandate at last election; first term; previous Washington experience; oratorical skills; competent senior White House staff; crises.

40 A term used to refer to a presidency characterised by the misuse and abuse of power and high-handedness in dealing with Congress.

41 Arthur Schlesinger.

42 Increased use of war-making powers; excessive secrecy; high-handedness in dealing with Congress; illegal activity; the failure of the traditional checks and balances to work effectively.

43 Lyndon Johnson and Richard Nixon.

44 Johnson was forced to decide not to stand for re-election in 1968; Nixon was forced to resign in 1974; as Ford pointed out, 'Our Constitution works', including its checks and balances; by the late 1970s there was much talk of an 'imperilled presidency' which was weak and ineffective.

45 War Powers Act.

Chapter 8 The Supreme Court

1 Nine.

2 The president.

3 By the Senate, simple majority required.

4 For life, or until they voluntarily retire.

5 Federal Appeal Court judges.

6 Strict constructionist: a justice of the Supreme Court who interprets the Constitution in a strict, literal or conservative fashion; loose constructionist: a justice of the Supreme Court who interprets the Constitution in a loose or liberal fashion.

7 Strict: Roberts, Scalia, Thomas, Alito; loose: Ginsburg, Breyer, Sotomayor, Kagan.

8 Swing justice.

9 The power of the Supreme Court to declare acts of Congress, or actions of the executive — or acts or actions of state governments — unconstitutional, and thereby null and void.

10 Through the Supreme Court decision in *Marbury* v. *Madison* (1803).

11 (a) Judicial activism: an approach to judicial decision making which holds that a judge should use his or her position to promote desirable social ends; (b) judicial restraint: an approach to judicial decision making which holds that a judge should defer to the legislative and executive branches and should put great stress on the precedent established in previous Court decisions.

12 14th Amendment.

13 (a) Substantive due process: the requirement that (the substance of) the law be administered fairly, reasonably and constitutionally; (b) procedural due process: the requirement that the process of the law must be fair.

14 (a) Civil rights: positive acts of government designed to protect persons against arbitrary or discriminatory treatment by government or individuals; (b) civil liberties: those liberties that guarantee the protection of persons, expression and property from arbitrary interference by the government.

15 The Court is making decisions in politically important and controversial matters of public policy; its members are appointed by a politician (the president) and confirmed by other politicians (senators).

16 The Court ruled that in terms of rights of political speech (and therefore making financial donations to political campaigns), business corporations have the same rights as individuals, thereby overturning key provisions of the 2002 Bipartisan Campaign Reform Act.

17 The Court stated for the first time that, in its interpretation, the 2nd Amendment right to 'keep and bear arms' is an individual, rather than merely a collective, right.

18 *Gideon* v. *Wainwright*: the Court interpreted the 14th Amendment as guaranteeing the right to legal representation; *Miranda* v. *Arizona*: the Court interpreted the 5th Amendment right to remain silent as extending to the right to be reminded of that right when arrested.

19 Court has ruled that execution of mentally retarded criminals and those who committed their crime when under 18 is unconstitutional.

20 *Gratz* v. *Bollinger* (2003): the Court ruled that the University of Michigan's affirmative action-based undergraduate admissions programme was unconstitutional because it was too 'mechanistic'; *Parents Involved in Community Schools Inc.* v. *Seattle School District No. 1* (2007) and *Meredith* v. *Jefferson County (Kentucky) Board of Education* (2007): the Court declared it unconstitutional to assign students to public schools solely for the purpose of achieving racial balance.

21 This was the first time the Court had declared that a specific abortion procedure could be banned and made no exception for the health of the woman, although it did provide an exception if the life of the mother was threatened.

22 (i) The Senate confirms all Supreme Court appointments; (ii) the House can impeach justices and the Senate try them and, if they are found guilty by a two-thirds majority, it can remove them from office; (iii) Congress can alter the number of justices on the Court; (iv) Congress can initiate constitutional amendments, thereby seeking to overturn judgments of the Court with which it disagrees.

23 Supporting: George W. Bush over *Zelman* v. *Simmons-Harris* in 2002; criticising: George H. W. Bush over flag-burning in 1990, or Barack Obama over *Citizens United* v. *FEC* in 2010.

24 One of: (i) having ruled in 1989 in *Stanford* v. *Kentucky* that states could execute 16- and 17-year-old offenders, reversed in 2003 (*Roper* v. *Simmons*), stating that such executions were unconstitutional; (ii) in 2000 (*Stenberg* v. *Carhart*), the Court declared a Nebraska state law prohibiting late-term abortions to be unconstitutional, but in 2007 (*Gonzales* v. *Carhart*) it upheld an almost identical federal law.

am practice answers and quick quizzes at **www.therevisionbutton.co.uk/myrevisionnotes**